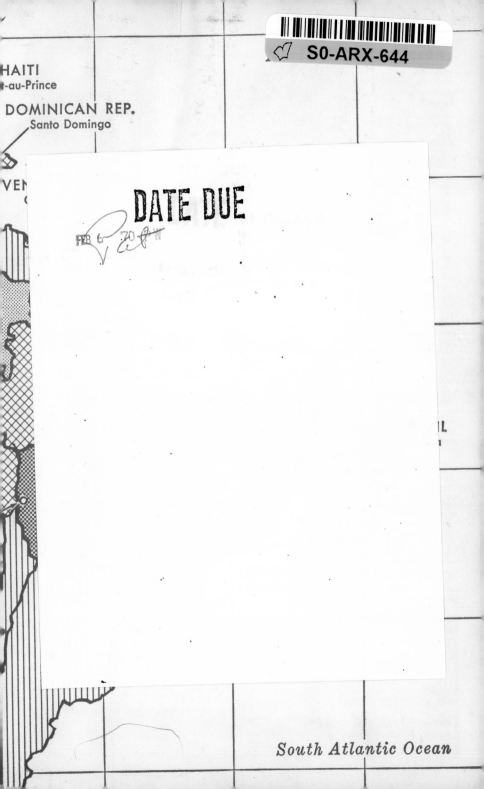

HAITI
t-au-Prince

DOMINICAN REP.
Santo Domingo

VEN

IL

South Atlantic Ocean

Latin America
The Eleventh Hour

By Gary MacEoin

CERVANTES
COMMUNIST WAR ON RELIGION
NOTHING IS QUITE ENOUGH

‡−‡−LATIN AMERICA
The Elevneth Hour

it isnt that late

Gary MacEoin

P. J. KENEDY & SONS
NEW YORK

Contents

Acknowledgment

A considerable part of the material on which this book is based has appeared in articles I have written over several years for *The Sign*, and I want to thank the editors of that thoughtful magazine for asking the questions for which I have tried to formulate answers. My wife's great help in assembling data during various field trips in Latin America was equaled by her patience during the trying incubation period of the manuscript. The many others who provided information, corrected errors, improved perspectives and suggested fuller meanings include John J. Considine, Wilfredo Guinea, John M. McGhee, Albert J. Nevins, Caroline Pezzullo, Josefina de Roman, Gerard Thormann, and Ramon Yllaramendy. I thank them all.

Foreword ·

Our stereotype of Latin America contains one abiding serene image in a kaleidoscope of comic-opera revolutions. It is the siesta-loving, fiesta-loving peasant frittering a perpetual summer away in the shade of his sombrero. Ambivalently, we envy him his leisure while bemoaning his neglect of his opportunities. But we're not really worried. It makes no great difference to us, one way or the other. We can count him with us when the chips are down, and anyway, there are always the marines.

Not a single element in the picture remains valid. Everyone of us must by now know that Latin America has had in recent years at least one revolution which is for real, and that this revolution has hurt us and is hurting us. It may not long be alone. If we do not know, we should know that the Latin American peasant has little time or taste for siesta or fiesta. He is fully occupied in a crushing, hopeless, unending grind, the struggle to stay alive and fill the hungry bellies of his many children.

And, most of all, Latin America matters to us. It is not merely that we cannot be sure of our prosperity if a slum develops in our backyard, though this too is true. More immediately, almost a quarter of the foreign trade on which four million United States workers depend directly for their livelihood is with Latin America. More than a quarter of our direct foreign investments of thirty billion dollars is in Latin America. In time of emergency, we are absolutely dependent on Latin America for many strategic raw materials and equally essential food supplies. Her land mass constitutes our southern defence, and our vulnerability would be tremendously increased if she were hostile or even negatively neutral.

Every day brings a new demonstration of the reality of these facts, which North Americans find it so hard to assimilate. In the past few years, a fifth of our total investment in Latin America has been confiscated without compensation in Cuba. The cessation of trade with that island has likewise wiped out a fifth of our entire trade with Latin America, representing the liquidation of the source of livelihood of several hundred thousand United States workers. And as even Khrushchev has been kind enough to remind us, the DEW warning line in northern Canada is no longer enough to protect us against nuclear warheads. Soviet rockets can now hit us from the other direction, across the South Pole and over the Latin American hemisphere.

What we seem to find most difficult of all to understand or to accept is that our problems with Latin America have scarcely begun, to understand that we are confronted with a society no longer static, a society recently and with revolutionary speed subjected to tremendous new forces—many of them generated by us—which are cracking the old structures and causing them to totter, so that it is futile to oppose the change. Our alternatives are to channel that change constructively, a task which will require effort and sacrifice such as we have till now resisted; or to let it develop away from us, so that it will destroy Latin America and surely destroy us too.

Such is the theme of this book, which reflects the fruits of eighteen years of involvement in and affection for Latin America. It attempts to review not only how things are in this vast and vital part of the world, but how they got the way they are, and how they can be renewed. If it is an indictment, it is an indictment of institutions that were once good but have ceased to be adequate. If it expresses concern that so little has been done, it also expresses belief that what must be done can be done, and confidence that it will be done.

G. MacE.

+ − + − *1*

+ − + − *Latin America in Eruption*

PEOPLE CONSTITUTE THE WARNING, THE
challenge and the hope of Latin America. Hungry children growing faster than anywhere else in the world form the most dynamic
element in an explosive situation. They sound the death knell of
an order that has outlived its usefulness. They proclaim the ur-
gency of, while providing an essential factor for, the efficient exploitation of the region's natural resources.

By Latin America, I mean the entire continent south of the
United States. Its land area is approximately two and one half
times that of the United States. It had 23 million people in 1810,
63 million in 1900, 166 million in 1950. It caught up with the
United States and Canada combined in 1955, when each had
about 183 millions. With its more rapid rate of increase (2.5 per

cent to 1.7 per cent), Latin America is now ahead, and extends its lead each year. By 1980, the population is expected to be double that of 1950. By the year 2000, it may reach or exceed 500 million.

The figure is not in itself alarming, for population density in Latin America is only slightly more than that of Africa, one-sixth that of Asia, and less than one-ninth that of Europe. Resources, while far from fully evaluated, are more than adequate to provide vastly higher than current living levels for all inhabitants now or in the calculable future. South America, for example, is estimated to have four times as much cultivable land per head of population as Asia, and half as much again as Europe. The growth rate, nevertheless, is a gravely complicating factor. Economic development must be stepped up to a tempo that will provide acceptable living levels not just for those whose standards are today totally inadequate but for a much bigger number. How low those levels are is indicated by a single statistic. Latin American production of goods and services is only 15 per cent that of North America.

Population distribution is far from uniform. The Amazon forest and Southern Argentina and Chile are among the world's least populated areas, while dense concentrations exist in the Caribbean and on the coasts of South America. Some big cities, too, have quite abnormal concentrations. Nearly half Uruguay's population lives in Montevideo—one-third that of Argentina in Buenos Aires, and one-fourth that of Chile in Santiago. Latin America has three of this continent's six biggest cities: Buenos Aires (5.6 million), Mexico City (4.7 million), and São Paulo (3.7 million).

Latin America's population is the world's youngest. Of every ten people, four are under the age of fifteen, a fact which helps to explain the stress on youth. Students usually exercise a tremendous influence on politics. Young men get quickly to the top in government and business if they start with the right introductions.

The rate of population growth is highest in Mexico, Central

America and tropical South America, less rapid in the densely populated islands of the Caribbean, and slowest in the temperate south of South America, where the population is mainly white, and where the living standards and age pyramids are more similar to those of Europe. The increase anticipated over the next fifty years is fourfold for the first area, threefold for the second, and only twofold for the third, in which current population density is generally very low.

Latin America's great empty areas open to agricultural exploitation do not serve as a buffer for the growing millions. Population tends to be bunched, often in mountain valleys along the historic discovery routes and at elevations which were healthy when malaria plagued the low tropics. Political control by the small upper class prevents the distribution of the big estates which often lie close at hand. Accordingly, while a hundred million workers and their families—more than half of Latin America's population—lacks enough to eat and enough to wear, they are not in a position to grow the food and fiber they desperately need. On the contrary, the situation gets worse each year. During the 1950's, the population increased by 45 per cent, but food production by only 32 per cent.

Meanwhile, surplus agricultural labor moves to the cities, where industry, because of its low rhythm of development, does not need it. In the next fifteen years, the labor force will increase by sixty-five million, but at the current rate of expansion the economy will absorb only a fifth of these new workers. In consequence, we can anticipate the further expansion of the huge slum suburbs which mushroom around the cities, peopled by unemployed and underemployed, evidencing and aggravating the violent social maladjustments.

The population explosion is introducing other stresses. For example, the non-white population is experiencing the greatest increase, becoming more important in relation to the white. In its foreign relations, likewise, Latin America is growing conscious of the value of manpower. The lower growth rate of the United States tends to increase Latin America's relative importance in world affairs. Forty years from now, its manpower may be twice ours.

It may be misleading, however, to talk about Latin America as an entity, still less as a force, without first explaining in more detail what is meant. While Latin America is much more than a geographic description for a group of neighboring countries, the region includes extremely diverse social, economic, cultural and human elements. Uruguay, for example, is no more like Peru than Switzerland is like Spain, or than Denmark is like Sicily.

Language is one of the elements dividing Latin Americans. Putting aside the small numbers of English and French-speaking communities in the Caribbean, a major distinction must be made between the one-third of Latin Americans whose official language is Portuguese (the Brazilians) and the two-thirds whose official language is Spanish.

I do not think that nearly enough attention has been given to the differences between these two groups whom we lump together as Latin Americans. I do not suggest that language is the cause of the differences, for many other factors are present, but I do think that the differences exist and are quite startling. One is in the form of government. While the constitutions of many Spanish-speaking countries of Latin America make them federal republics in legal form, all are in fact highly centralist and unitary, while Brazil alone shows in practice truly federative characteristics.

Also distinctive of Brazil is a kind of frontier attitude to life, reminiscent of an earlier period in the United States, often a tough, get-rich-quick attitude, impatient with tradition. Brazil does in fact still have an expanding frontier, a territory as big as the continental United States but with only one-third the population, almost all concentrated in a relatively small part of the national territory. As employees, I have found Brazilians aggressive, impatient to advance, ready to experiment, rather like New Yorkers; while other Latin Americans remind me more of Canadians, polite, self-effacing, fond of routine.

I always remember a trifling incident which I consider significant. It concerns an Ecuadorian who worked for me in a professional capacity. I went to considerable trouble to show him how he could rationalize a routine operation, speed up his production and raise his earning capacity. He listened with infinite politeness, nodding his head and indicating approval as I proceeded. However, when I ended, he asked permission to comment. As he spoke, his emotions got the better of him, the only time during a long and happy relationship that this happened. If, he told me, the choices that confronted him were more money or working at his own tempo, he preferred to work at his own tempo.

This story, I think, throws a small light on the area in which most misunderstandings and bitterness begin in relations between Latin Americans and North Americans. While, no doubt, there are political and economic causes for some differences, the objective fact is that the true interests of the two regions are parallel. But our divergent scales of values develop enmities and fears where there is no reason for them.

It is hardly necessary to add that the difference in emotional response as between Latin Americans who speak Spanish and those who speak Portuguese is not nearly as great as that between Latin Americans and North Americans. Culture values and customs are far apart, and we can easily cause offense by doing what to us seems normal and natural in given circumstances, as I shall try to illustrate by a recent experience. I was visiting in South America with a small group of United States college students, and

we were invited to a reception arranged in our honor by some
friends at their club in a small city deep in the Andes.

The reception was scheduled from 7 to 9, but through no fault
of ours it was almost nine when we arrived. We had been out in
the country on a trip that lasted several hours beyond schedule.
Embarrassed, we changed quickly and hurried to our appointment
without having eaten since noon. The boys were hungry, and
someone got the idea that they would order, and of course pay
for, sandwiches at the club short-order counter. Fortunately, I over-
heard the discussion and persuaded them—with no little difficulty
—that no greater offense to our host was possible than to suggest
that his hospitality left anything to be desired. Starve to death, if
you must, I urged them, but show no sign of hunger until your
host decides to serve food. And right enough, on towards mid-
night, food began to appear, and the party continued merrily until well after one in the morning.

The following day I was recounting to an intimate friend among
the Latin Americans who had been present how I had been able to
save the honor of the United States. He found it difficult to com-
prehend how the idea of buying food at a party could even occur
to anyone with a shred of breeding, then added sadly: "But you
disappoint me, Gary. I thought you knew us better than not to
realize what a horrible gaffe was in fact committed last night."

I tried to recall every circumstance but still could not figure this
one out. We had arrived two hours late. We had stayed four hours
beyond our invitation. If my guests back home did that kind of
thing to me, I'd feel a grievance. But I knew that was nothing.
My friend agreed.

"That was nothing," he said. "Nobody is upset about when you
come or when you go. But don't you recall? While the boys were
dancing with the very charming daughters of your hosts, one of

those characters took off his jacket and went about in his shirt sleeves."

It was my turn to be amazed. It was true that one of the boys had in fact taken off his jacket. But it was a warm evening, and he was very properly dressed otherwise, with collar and tie and a long-sleeved shirt, and they were a crowd of young people having properly supervised fun. But my friend insisted. "I'd as soon think of appearing in bathing trunks," he said heatedly.

I'm not suggesting that the Latin Americans are right. Personally, I think that the attitude revealed by this episode was quite unreasonable, and that our greater informality and our concern if we keep others waiting represents a more normal and mature approach to social relations. The point I am making is that we must recognize the existence of such differences, and their subjective importance, and we must work hard to identify them and adjust to them.

The people with whom the visitor comes in contact will speak either Spanish or Portuguese, according to the country. But many Latin Americans speak neither language. They are the Indians, the greater part—though not by any means all—of whom have in the course of four centuries come more or less within the sphere of European culture and have undergone some degree of racial intermingling with the descendants of the conquistadores. Quechua is spoken by about 60 per cent of all Peruvians, and most of those who speak it do not speak any other language. This group is growing faster than any other in the country, so that the proportion of Quechua-speakers—all, of course, illiterate—is rising. Quechua is also the language of many Bolivians. In some countries, such as Mexico, Peru and Bolivia, the Indian predominates in the general population. In a few, like Argentina and Uruguay, the European racial strains predominate.

Our difficulties in establishing effective communication and understanding with Spanish or Portuguese-speaking Latin Americans who share the same basic culture derived from Western Europe as ourselves, are as nothing compared with the problem of getting to know the Indian and learning what are the things that matter to him. As will become apparent in the following pages, one of the principal tragedies of Latin America has been the failure to reach an understanding with the indigenous inhabitants. From the first ' arrival of the Spaniards, there has existed an unbridged chasm, and the absence of a meeting of minds has been a primary cause of the decay and collapse of the Indian way of life without its replacement by any other vital social form.

So complete has been the breakdown of Indian society, that, notwithstanding considerable rhetoric in Mexico to the contrary, today the Indian can move only toward integration into European culture. It is true that before the arrival of the European colonizers the Indians created their own great cultures, such as the Maya in Mexico and Guatemala between the fifth and twelfth centuries of the Christian era, the Aztec in Mexico from the fourteenth century to the sixteenth, and the Inca on the west coast of South America from Argentina to Colombia from the eleventh century to the sixteenth. But the Indian of today retains hardly a memory of this great past, even when he lives among its magnificent ruins. Instead, the word *Indian* is merely descriptive of scores and hundreds of unrelated groups which do not today and did not at any past time share a common language, historical experience or religion.

Because the Indians represent so many isolated fragments, it is hard to make meaningful generalizations about them. They have been little studied, and many of the conclusions of researchers have been vitiated by the non-scientific approach of the sociologist or social anthropologist who found only what he was looking for.

I think, however, that it would be foolish to assume that the stolidity and passivity which have historically characterized the Indian can be counted on to maintain him indefinitely in a position of economic and social inferiority. The recent and current Bolivian experiences (to be discussed later), suggest quite the contrary. The Bolivian Indians who got a very slight training as minor leaders in the Chaco Wars with Paraguay quickly revealed their initiative on their return home and converted into a struggle for Indian land rights what had begun as a middle-class attempt to muscle in on the machinery and prerogatives of government. Since that time, Communist propagandists in the highlands of Bolivia and bordering Peru have developed a well-trained and thoroughly indoctrinated Indian leadership.

Communist infiltration of these Indian groups in the high Andes is one of the weirdest, least-documented, and potentially dangerous elements in the Latin American picture. As long ago as 1950, an American anthropologist established contact in Ecuador with leaders of a group of 30,000 Indians who described themselves as Communists. They did not know who Stalin was, where or what Russia was, or what Marx had said. But they felt that their landlords were exploiting them, and they wanted their own land. Communist agitators had done the rest.

Since that time, considerable Communist leadership has been developed from among the Indians themselves. José Rojas, an Indian from the valley of Cochabamba, who claims he speaks no Spanish although he lived for a time in Argentina, was elected to the Senate of Bolivia in 1956. He and people like him are thoroughly indoctrinated, and they are busily engaged in projecting dreams of a Communist Indian empire to rival that of their Inca forebears who ruled all these lands from Colombia to Argentina.

The social system which holds the unassimilated Indians at the bottom of the totem pole has existed with only minimal change for four centuries, so that it has become emotionally intolerable for those who enjoy the benefits of this relationship to contemplate any change. The point was illustrated for me recently in conversation with a friend who works as an organizer for the Christian trades unions in Peru, a conversation which also brought out the extent of the gulf between the thought processes and value judgments of the Indians and men of Western culture.

In reply to my query about the progress of unionization among Peruvian farm workers, he told me that both the Christian and the Socialist trades unions had made several attempts to organize the workers on the big estates. They had no particular difficulty in signing up enough people to justify their approach to the employer with a request for recognition and a series of demands for more money and better work conditions. In every case, the employer, who traditionally regards his peons as his chattels, refused absolutely to deal with a union. In due course a strike would follow. At first, there would be little bitterness. Gradually, however, the employer would begin to see that his production was being affected. He would then call the local military commander and request troops to protect his executives from threats of physical violence, a request which the commander was bound to honor.

"What happens next," concluded my friend, "may seem strange to you, but it is not only logical but inevitable for anyone who understands the psychology of our Indians. The Indian cannot withdraw under threat of physical force. This is a culture trait which caused much needless bloodshed during and since the Conquest. Faced by the guns of the soldiers, his only choice is to advance on them and be shot down. And that is how today the employers prevent the unionization of the Indians. They arrange for the army to shoot them down. We have had several examples in the past few years and the technique is not exclusive to our feudal landlords. One of the employers was a United States company."

That an alternative method of dealing with the Indians exists
has been demonstrated by an extraordinary experiment begun in
the Peruvian highlands under the direction of a Cornell University team in 1952. They took over a hacienda of 35,000 acres, on
which 1,850 Indians lived and worked. These people existed in
most deplorable conditions of health, education and housing. For
centuries they had never made a decision for themselves. The
Cornell people persuaded them that it was possible to change their
condition, that they could pull themselves up by their own efforts.
They started by showing how to increase the yields of crops, so
that a part could be sold to pay rent for the plots instead of the
traditional three days' unpaid labor weekly. Then they encouraged them to develop a school, to improve their homes, and finally
to take title to the hacienda and assume responsibility for its operation, paying to the government in taxes an amount equal to what
the hacienda would bring its owner in rent. This pilot operation
took less than ten years to reach a self-sustaining level, a striking
indication of the speed with which change can occur under opti-
mum conditions.

The real significance of the Cornell experiment lies in the fact
that the hacienda is the specific institution which maintains the
Indian in a condition of permanent inferiority and helplessness.
This method of land exploitation enables its owner to derive substantial wealth for himself by working a large extension of poorly
cared for land with big numbers of ill-paid workers and minimum
input of capital. The individual worker produces only slightly more
than is needed to keep him alive, but the landowner by multipli-
cation of the small surpluses of each of many workers does very
well when export prices for the products are good, and he can
survive intervals of low prices because he pays neither tax on his
land nor wages to his workers.

The system is, in consequence, extremely resilient and it has for

centuries resisted any major modifications. The original occupation and seizure of the lands of the Indians was justified by the
legal fiction that all rights had been vested in the crown by conquest. In 1511, just nineteen years after the first voyage of Colum-
bus, a system of tutelage known as *encomienda* was created over
the Indians. This provided that the Indians were free men, not
slaves, that they should be instructed in the Catholic faith, that
they could be compelled to work, provided that the work did not
interfere with their religious duties and that it was profitable to
themselves as well as to the state, that it was proportioned to their
strength and for reasonable hours. In addition, it was declared that
they should have their own homes and should have time to culti-
vate their own lands.

The fact that the encomienda system quickly degenerated, contrary to the intention of those who had devised it, into a technique
for subjugating the Indians instead of civilizing them, must not
blind us to the extraordinary benefits which the Conquest did in
fact confer on what is now Latin America, including the assimi-
lation and uplift of the substantial proportion of Indians whose
blood runs today in the veins of upper and middle-class Latin
Americans. Among such advances may be listed the creation of the
first diocese in Puerto Rico in 1511, and of the first university
school in Mexico in 1524. Six years later came a full-fledged university in Santo Domingo and a printing press in Mexico City.
The Catholic Church was solidly established in all the Spanish
and Portuguese territories with the creation of dioceses and ecclesiastical provinces. The Jesuits in Paraguay organized an astonish-
ing system of Christian socialism which brought the material,
moral and cultural benefits of European civilization to the Indians within the framework of their own language and way of life.

By the end of the eighteenth century, thirteen universities were
flourishing. Architecture had more than a century of achievements,

starting with the great American baroque cathedrals of Mexico, Quito and Lima. Public works, irrigation and drainage projects, sewers, navigable canals, were expanding, especially in Mexico. Humboldt reported at the end of the eighteenth century that cultivation of the land was on the level of the best in France, that livestock production was notable, that the trades were flourishing. An English traveler said the cotton, woolen and linen factories produced fabrics better than any in England or France.

What might have happened, if the forces brought into action by Spain in the New World had been allowed to develop in a straight line, can be only a subject for speculation. I am not suggesting that the original blueprint was perfect. The early explorers were obsessed with the idea of extracting mineral wealth rather than settling on the land, and many of them forced the Indians to work beyond their powers and under horrible conditions. Administration was never Spain's strong point. The wrongdoer could generally laugh at the excellent laws promulgated by the Council of the Indies.

But there was no general plan to wipe out the Indians or confine them to reservations. The law resolutely refused to countenance the many efforts of the colonizers to reduce them to slavery. It remained official policy to develop them to a condition of full equality with the whites, but unfortunately there was never a true meeting of the minds as to what this meant or how it ought to be effected. The surprise of the Spaniards at the variety of peoples and cultures they found in America was extreme, and one of the great errors they made was to identify in their own minds the nature of these cultures with the pagan ceremonies and superstitions in which the Indians expressed them. And if they got a warped idea about the Indians, it was nothing to the warped image which the Indians for their part formed of the Spaniards. They were overwhelmed by this visit of the gods, of gods with magic powers. They refused to think of the Spaniards as people like themselves, thus making communication and understanding impossible. They reached common ground only in the Catholic missions, where alone the Indians prospered and multiplied. Unfortunately, however, these missions were able to play only a relatively marginal role, and their work was interrupted before it had put down roots.

In addition to the obstacle of mutual misunderstanding, a major reason for Spain's failure was her inability to support the burden she had assumed. Too great a part of the total effort was devoted to defending the over-extended lines of communication from the attacks of European enemies. In the political area, the breakdown came with the French Revolution. When Napoleon invaded Spain in 1808, a total collapse in that country's internal organization occurred. The first revolts occurred in Venezuela, Argentina, Chile and Mexico, not against Spain as such, but against a government in Spain controlled by a foreign invader. The process, once begun, could not be reversed, and so the colonies were launched on their own with most inadequate equipment, by historical accident rather than a will to be free. Not that any other possibility then existed, for Spain was by this time so broken as no longer to have the potential to continue direction of the former colonies, even had they themselves been willing to extend the period of tutelage.

But a more profound if less obvious disruption of Latin America's evolution had already occurred. In the first instance, Spain had taken very seriously the task she had assumed of converting the Indians to Catholicism, a work conducted by the major religious orders, Augustinians, Franciscans, Dominicans and Jesuits. Close cooperation was maintained between Church and State, and in practice the Church was responsible for social, cultural and religious activities, including the development of the universities. The missionaries performed a most valuable linguistic function, making dictionaries and grammars of the Indian languages. They built roads, aqueducts and churches, with the help of Indians whom they trained in the necessary skills. They fought nobly, beginning with the famous Dominican, Bartolomé de las Casas, to protect the Indians from exploitation. The Jesuits who started the Paraguay Reductions went so far as to get official authorization to live in the separate communities of the Indians, removed from "the evil influences" of the Spaniards.

For reasons which had nothing whatever to do with the religious situation in Latin America but were dictated by political considerations in Europe, the Jesuits were expelled in 1767. The resulting vacuum was the greater because the other religious orders had declined considerably in numbers and religious spirit. In Chile, for example, there were 400 Jesuits for a total population of 400,000, one priest per thousand inhabitants, which is about the same proportion as in Spain today.

No attempt was made to fill the vacuum, and in consequence a cultural and religious anemia set in which still continues. Catholicism had been firmly established and this fundamental fact was never reversed. But it quickly became characterized by illiteracy of the masses, a shortage of vocations to the priesthood, a lack of religious instruction among the intellectuals, a revival of pagan superstitions and a development of spiritist and occultist movements.

The condition was compounded by the events connected with the movement for independence half a century later. Spain and Portugal had been granted by the Holy See the same right of patronage they enjoyed at home. Bishops were named by the king and confirmed by the Pope. Almost all bishops were accordingly Europeans, and they opposed the revolutionaries, the more so because of the "liberal" ideology, with strong overtones of Freemasonry and anticlericalism derived from the French Revolution, which characterized the leaders of the separatist movements. The new republics for their part insisted on taking over all the rights of the former regimes, including the right of patronage. Spain and Portugal, which did not recognize the independence of the new states for a long time, used their influence at Rome to prevent admission of such a claim. In consequence, many dioceses remained for years without bishops.

In this atmosphere the universities were secularized and made totally subject to state control, and gradually secondary and primary education suffered a like fate, with elimination of religious instruction from education in many countries. In many places, the property of the Church was seized, often without any adequate provision being made for the upkeep of the charitable and health services maintained by the Church. Religious orders were secularized. Former checks on exploitation of the Indians disappeared. And gradually the negative attitudes of the ruling classes toward the Church, which come as such a surprise to those who simply think of Latin America as a Catholic culture (which it basically is), formed and hardened into traditions.

The encomienda system, which in turn developed into the hacienda, made the Indian effectively the serf of the landowner, in spite of the contrary intention of the legislators, and such he remains. In the year 1959, when Maryknoll missionaries from the United States sparked the building of a village in a mountain parish in Peru and a number of Indians left neighboring haciendas to live and work there, the local landlords formed a posse of armed horsemen and drove the peons by force back to their farms.

The benefits of the hacienda system must, nevertheless, be recognized. Where it was established, it enabled the Indians to survive. This was a better fate than befell them in North America or in those parts of Latin America where they were—again in disregard of the protective laws—forced to work in extraction of minerals.

Work in mines was particularly onerous for the Indians, and in many areas they began to die off rapidly. To replace them, Africans were brought as slaves from the sixteenth to the nineteenth century. They form a substantial part of the population in Brazil, in the port cities of Venezuela, Colombia and Ecuador, in the islands of the Caribbean and on the adjoining mainland. The descendants of these Africans have been more fully integrated into the general population than has occurred in the United States. They still form the lowest economic class in the cities, as the Indians do in the country, and suffer similar social discrimination. But the discrimination is not based on race as such, a factor permitting more fluidity than in the United States as well as a more rapid breaking down of barriers when economic advancement occurs. Race discrimination is not supported by legal provisions or devices anywhere in Latin America.

Until the countries of Latin America gained their freedom during the first quarter of the last century, European immigration into them was from Spain and Portugal only. During the second and third quarters, a number of Irish and Scots settled in Chile and Argentina, and at about the same time many Germans went to south Brazil and south Chile. The beginnings of this century saw substantial Italian immigration into Argentina and Uruguay, and a new wave of immigration from Spain to many countries. There was also a smaller movement from Japan, mainly to Brazil, and from Holland. Small-scale immigration from Europe and Japan continues.

Emigration from Latin America is directed exclusively toward the United States. The two main groups are Puerto Ricans who concentrate in New York, and Mexican farm workers in the southwestern states. There is, in addition, a continuous trickle of white-collar workers and intellectuals from all parts of Latin America into New York and a few other United States cities. The socialization of

Cuba following the Castro take-over caused an unprecedented move of Cubans, mostly of the upper and middle classes, to Florida and New York.

Historically, the settlers came to North America to create a new world and a new culture. Leaving Europe to escape religious or political persecution, they arrived in a frame of emotional revolt and rejection of the past. The colonizers of Latin America set out with entirely different intentions. The official policy, the implementation of which was sought not only by the clergy but by many lay leaders, was to transplant the religion and culture of Europe and impose them on the natives of America. Even the adventurers, with less worthy motives, thought of themselves as crossing the ocean simply to make a quick fortune and bring it back to Europe in the form of gold or other precious metals. They were not planning to settle and carve out a new life, though many of them did so when the dreams of fortune evaporated.

The results of these two different colonizing intentions are clearly visible today. While the United States has a culture and outlook extremely different from Europe, Latin America is less original. The former native culture was indeed as thoroughly destroyed in Latin as in North America, leaving as active cultural elements only those originating in Europe. However, the impact from Europe was affected by all the vagaries of European politics and social currents which have already been indicated. The militant Counter-Reformation Catholicism of Spain dominated the early period, to be gradually eclipsed and in the nineteenth century almost completely replaced by French social and cultural patterns, which included anticlericalism and irreligion.

From the time of the expulsion of the Jesuits and the decline of influence of the Catholic Church, however, the earlier efforts to absorb the Indians culturally came almost to a halt. In consequence, a great part of the population is still either entirely or to a major extent uninfluenced by the culture of Europe, so that often only a relatively small proportion of the inhabitants of a country constitute its culturally active elements. This group will think of itself as constituting the entire community, speaking and planning without considering the non-integrated population as a part of the total national problem or concern.

This fact must be borne well in mind when discussing with Latin Americans such problems as democracy, voting rights, literacy, or social welfare benefits. In all good faith, they will offer estimates and even statistics based only on the culturally active population, leaving aside the inert masses. Often this means that the discussion is in reality concerned with the city dwellers to the practical exclusion of the rural inhabitants. Reflecting the age-long tradition of the Mediterranean, the city is still for the Latin American the state. Once we go south of the Rio Grande, the farm vote ceases to exist. And so, if a Latin American is talking about the workers or the dispossessed masses, or about pensions or separation benefits, he is most likely only thinking of the city and of factory workers, even though in fact they represent but a small percentage of the have-nots in his country.

+ − + − *The Have-Nots*

IT IS NOT EASY TO ACHIEVE A TRUE UN-
derstanding of underdevelopment without substantial first hand experience. To read about it or even to see isolated aspects provides
no real appreciation of the complicated causes which make it
self-perpetuating. When, however, you explore far enough, you
discover that you are dealing with a vicious circle.

"You cannot offer school lunches unless you have schools," a
Brazilian economist recently commented, "and you cannot have
schools unless you prevent the children from dying of disease and
malnutrition before they reach school age. And this in turn will
not be possible until we can create economic activity in the vast
depressed areas, provide jobs and help people to live like human
beings."

To pursue the same example, if you go into a village and find that only a third of the children are at school, you will think this is a pretty grim situation but not too hard to remedy. Even if the school is only a shack and contains neither desks nor books, these are things that money can quickly supply. However, it becomes more complicated when you establish that the village teacher is himself practically illiterate, having never gone beyond grade school and lacking any pedagogic training. Teachers are in charge of classes and even of schools in Latin America today whose sole academic qualification is one year of grade schooling. There are not enough trained teachers because there are not enough training colleges or enough qualified professors to teach in them. Not one teacher in ten has reached what we in the United States would regard as an acceptable minimum level of preparation for his job.

Here you may think we are back at money, and in a sense this is true. But money will not be forthcoming, even if it is available, unless education has an economic function. However, for most of these village children, it has none. Learning to read and write will not add to their earning capacity within the static economy of their village. In the curious social structure of a country like Peru or Ecuador, the function of the Indian is to work on the land of his *patrón,* using the most primitive tools and unimproved methods. So thoroughly is this understood that if he sends his children to school, the teacher will not waste their time by instructing them in reading and writing but will put them to work in his garden. Naturally enough, the Indian has the intelligence to see that his children would be as profitably engaged in cultivating his own garden as that of the teacher, and so their academic career reaches a quick end. Nor is drop-out confined to Indians. In Colombia, of each hundred rural children who start school only one completes four years.

Let us assume, however, that an unusual child perseveres for the full five years which constitute the grade school course in most countries, and learns reading, writing and arithmetic. He now starts at the age of twelve to work with his father in the fields. He lives in a home without a chair, a table, a window, a lamp. It has no books or newspapers. There is neither opportunity nor inducement for him to practice the basic learning he has acquired. Ten or fifteen years later, when it is time for his own children to start their schooling, he is functionally illiterate. He is no more able to help them than his parents were to help him.

I could go on and on, but I shall merely note one additional complication in such countries as Mexico, Guatemala, Ecuador, Peru and Bolivia, with a high Indian population. The school language is not even the language of the home for many children, and some of them may understand only an obscure Indian dialect which their teacher does not speak.

I mentioned just now homes without chairs, tables, windows or lamps. I was in one such recently. It had mud walls and a palm-leaf roof. It consisted of two small rooms, with an open lean-to outside for cooking. Not only did it not have tables or chairs, but it had no beds or other furniture. The only belongings, apart from the clothes the members of the family wear, are some sacks to spread under them on the dirt floor at night, and a few pots and pans for cooking the plantains, beans and corn on which they live.

The head of this family, Gerardo Román, is well off compared to many of his neighbors. For over a year, he has had steady work at seven dollars a week on a nearby farm. But in all his thirty-eight years, he has never had a chance to go to school, nor has he ever made enough money to give his wife and their five children the basic things they need. The children do not go to school. Like their parents before them, they lack the clothes, the books, the place to study.

Throughout Latin America there are millions of Gerardo Románs—men attached to big estates, who give up to three days' unpaid labor each week to a landlord, plus other services, in return for a few acres to grow the family's food. They sow and harvest by hand, as in biblical times, using little fertilizer, though the soil is worn out. Seed has degenerated and gives low yields. Pesticides to protect plants from diseases are unknown to them. Insects and rodents eat more of the stored crop than does the family.

Gerardo Román and his wife Eloise have, however, made one major step into the twentieth century. They are conscious that they lack many things, which if they had them, would improve their life. Strange as it may seem, this is one of the toughest problems of underdevelopment. There is little one can do for people in the absence of identified needs. Humans do not automatically long for and strive for a shower, an automobile or a beach home. The only way they know how to live is how they live. Faced with unexpected improvement in their economic condition, they are most likely to spend their new wealth unwisely, perhaps anti-socially. Given living benefits which they have not consciously lacked, they will abuse them and feel no sense of gratitude toward those who gave them what they didn't want in the first place.

A trivial incident many years ago in the Caribbean illustrated this point for me in a way I shall never forget. A remarkable nun, just released from a Nazi internment camp, had been put in charge of an orphanage, and she was trying hard to modernize an extremely Victorian atmosphere. One day I called to see her, she was jubilant. She had persuaded her superiors to introduce a change they had considered excessive. The older girls were to be given more freedom in preparation for their leaving the orphanage. As a first step, they were moved to a separate dormitory, where each had a cubicle of her own, curtained off to give her some privacy, and furnished with a bed and chair.

She brought me to see the dormitory. But imagine her chagrin and my mystification to find all the curtains drawn back and all the chairs piled in a corner. The reason was very simple. These girls had come from homes similar to that of Gerardo Román, homes in which all lived together and slept together. They had no chairs and consequently no use for them, any more than they had for privacy. Even the beds were alien to them, though in the orphanage they had been drilled into using them, yet—curiously enough—not to the point of accepting a mattress, insisting rather on a base of wooden boards on a bed frame. And the acceptance of the bed was far from complete. A major activity of the nurses in the maternity ward of the hospital was getting the expectant mothers back into bed. At the first onset of labor pains, they took refuge under their beds and fought like wounded animals against anyone who tried to help them.

Such is the complexity of underdevelopment. I ran into another striking example of it recently deep in the Andes where I was searching for a suitable location to film some scenes of a film on the Peace Corps. It was easy to find locations showing absolutely primitive conditions, but I wanted also to include the home of a peasant family which had begun to improve its living conditions and which would illustrate what benefits can be anticipated from the kind of grass-roots help the Peace Corps is setting out to provide.

Following what seemed like a good lead, I travelled several hours by jeep and foot to the home of a farm laborer whose employer had built a new house for him a few years ago. The circumstances were interesting. The employer, a successful professional man, had a country home located on a long-neglected farm. He decided to rehabilitate the place and obtained from the agricultural extension services not only technical guidance but also recommendations and plans for workers' houses.

The technical guidance had been very successful. With a modest investment of money, the owner of the land had introduced new varieties of the crops grown on the farm, increased the use of fertilizer and modernized the cultivation practices, and was now making good profits. The new house for his workman, had, however, not turned out so well. The man had not wanted windows. The employer insisted, and they were installed. But immediately on occupation, the man closed them to exclude air and covered them over to exclude light. He was now living in a soundly constructed brick building, but otherwise the conditions were little better than in the former mud shack. The concrete floor was encrusted with dirt. The children were unwashed. The same stream near the house served for laundry, for sanitary arrangements and for drinking water.

A Latin American president recently summed up this complex problem of underdevelopment very well. "It is the inadequacy of state funds to support public education," he said, "to care for the public health, to form a network of communications between the scattered communities, to ensure adequate services to administer justice and maintain public order. It is maldistribution of the land, its low productivity, an impoverishing over-fragmentation and sterile concentration into excessively big holdings.

"It is low labor efficiency, lack of preparation for solving even elementary problems, absence of a professional and technical class to run government and business efficiently. It is the housing shortage, low salaries, malnutrition, little food, high-cost production in industry and agriculture, the wandering life of vast numbers of rural workers in search of an occasional day's work.

"It is the inability to buy, with the sole proceeds of the exportation of a single crop whose price fluctuates in the world markets, the machines and goods the country does not produce. It is the open or hidden unemployment of millions who leave the land that cannot support them and go to cities in search of uncertain work. It is the hovels, the panhandling, the neglected children, the juvenile delinquency of these big cities."

Let me try to sketch in greater detail some of the generalizations. I must necessarily use figures and percentages, but I do want to stress the fact that part of the problem of underdevelopment and consequently of Latin America is not only a lack of statistics but a lack of the frame of mind which makes statistics possible. Considerable improvement has occurred in this field in recent years, but the sudden growth has been a mixed blessing. Some bizarre results have been produced by an understandable desire to ape the statistical coverage of more advanced countries combined with an equally understandable urge on the part of each country to show more progress than its neighbors. One consequence is that all statistics must be treated with reserve. Or to repeat a wonderful remark once made by a Central American intellectual, "Statistics in Latin America are poetry."

Besides, many of the phenomena will not emerge from crude statistics. What meaning is there in a given proportion of teachers to pupils, if—as we have seen—a teacher is not necessarily someone trained to teach? Similarly, the levels of literacy would provide a fairly good indication of the extent of culture penetration if it were possible to establish with a degree of accuracy what these levels are. But what was said above about pupils who are not admitted to classes and about loss of functional literacy from disuse suggests how hard this is.

In a general way, it is estimated that half the population of Latin America cannot read or write. A few countries, notably Uruguay and Argentina, have high literacy levels. Others, as Haiti and Guatemala, are admittedly low. But no one can say for sure, nor is there even an agreed definition of literacy, which some countries consider present if a person can sign his name. Frequently, the official statistics are demonstrably inaccurate. Cuba, for example, claimed 78 per cent literacy during the late 1950's, when little more than half the children of school age were enrolled in either public or private schools.

Or let us go back to the other point already touched on: the quality of the teachers. Colombia ranks above the middle point on the scale of Latin American countries in terms of most aspects of its development. It has an outstanding reputation for its cultural achievements. It so happens that in 1960 Colombia's educational authorities got a better than ordinary glimpse of the teacher picture in their country. The technique used was rather interesting. A questionnaire was sent to all teachers in the public schools, national, departmental and municipal, and salary payment was withheld until the questionnaire was returned.

It can be assumed that some of the respondents shaded their academic ratings in their own favor, but let us take them as they described themselves. Twenty-one per cent of Colombia's 32,798 teachers had studied in a teacher training college, but only 11 per cent had completed teacher training. Another 34 per cent had started high school, but only 4 per cent had finished. Passing over some other forms of teacher preparation at approximately the junior high school level, we find at the bottom of the pile 5,432 teachers, nearly 17 per cent of the total, who did not themselves go beyond grade school. Fifteen of them claimed only one year of grade school.

Further analysis brings out other aspects of the vicious circle. Partly as cause and partly as effect of the inadequate professional preparation, the teachers' salaries are miserably low, dropping to 200 pesos a month, or less than a dollar a day. A skilled worker can do much better, and consequently only the least intelligent and enterprising continue as teachers. The good ones stay a year or two until they find a better opening. For men, the profession is particularly unattractive. They account for only 20 per cent of all teachers, and more than half of them are unmarried.

To complete the picture, these aspects must be correlated with the age composition of the population. While the percentage of the population under fourteen years of age is 22 in England and 27 in the United States, it is 40 in Latin America. In some countries the percentage of young people is still growing, and in all, the absolute number of children of school age is growing and will continue to grow with the rise in population. In many countries, school construction and teacher formation lag behind population increase, so that literacy levels may fall in the near future, and certainly the number of illiterates, if not the percentage, is due to rise in many countries.

Extremes of wealth and poverty, with few people in the middle of the scale, constitute another aspect of underdevelopment. For Latin America as a whole, income per head of population averages not much more than $200, perhaps a tenth of the average for the United States. There are substantial variations from country to country and even greater ones between groups within different countries.

In agriculture, the income is usually much lower than in other sectors of the economy. The typical farm worker earns only a half or a third of his counterpart in industry, even when allowance is made for what he receives in kind or grows on his own plot of land. It is true that even in developed countries, the rural worker is usually the lowest paid, but he represents a much smaller proportion of the population. Farming occupies more than half of all Latin Americans, only 12 per cent of the inhabitants of the United States.

Both in agriculture and in other sectors of the economy, wealth is most unequally distributed. A young Chilean economist recently tried to explain this phenomenon to me, as it affects his country. "Our gross national product of approximately $500 per inhabitant, less than a fifth of the United States level," he said, "does not give a true index of the condition of the rural worker. While income inequalities in the order of one to twenty are usual in developed and semi-developed countries, the inequalities between the rich and poor in Chile approach the order of one to a hundred. Many rural families have incomes of thirty escudos ($27) monthly, while wealthy families will enjoy incomes of 2,500 escudos monthly. This family variation already exceeds eighty to one, and when you adjust for the bigger families of the poor, it rises on the individual level to a variation of a hundred to one.

"Because of this situation," my economist friend concluded, "I am afraid that the word *semideveloped*, which is now being used to describe the conditions of countries such as mine, gives a wrong connotation to people who look only at the over-all figures. Here we have rather two communities, one highly developed, well fed, living in luxury, the other underdeveloped, homeless, hungry, millions of people subsisting for a year on what an average United States middle class family will spend on a week-end trip."

This comment is applicable to most of Latin America. Everywhere you have extreme contrasts of wealth and poverty, not geographically separated, but side by side, in the shadow of each other, yet maintained in their parallel existences by the rigid organization of society. Taking the entire region, 20 per cent of the people enjoy 50 per cent of the income, the other 80 per cent having a per capita income of approximately $130 U. S. annually. In Chile, 38 per cent of the people get 76 per cent of the national income. In Colombia, 2.6 per cent of the people get 30 per cent. In Chile, the *inquilino* gets a family income of $200 to $300 a year, while his landlord's income runs between $50,000 and $200,000, none of which he plows back into the land to modernize his operation. His lavish way of life absorbs 64 per cent. Savings, invested outside agriculture and often outside the country, take a further 21 per cent, and only 14 per cent is captured by taxes. Corresponding percentages in England are 30, 27 and 42. In Peru, Lima's one million people receive more than half the national income, $450 per capita, while the other eight million Peruvians average less than $50 each per year.

Yet redistribution of the wealth would by itself solve little, because such per capita incomes do not suffice for basic human needs. In addition to a social reorganization to distribute the national wealth more equitably, there is needed an economic reorganization to increase the national income enormously. As already noted, Latin Americans, though slightly more numerous than North Americans, produce only fifteen per cent as much goods and services. Moreover, the gap is widening, because since 1945 their productivity has grown more slowly than ours. To change this situation will require specific reforms such as more geographic mobility, industrialization, emphasis on material achievement and a degree of material and social security where these do not now exist. Such prospects, however, are a mortal threat to the exclusive position of the very wealthy as also to the prematurely granted social security of the privileged class of industrial workers.

Hunger is another dimension of underdevelopment. Among dietary deficiencies in Latin America, the most widespread is a shortage of animal fats, extreme in all countries except Argentina, Uruguay and Paraguay, sparsely populated countries dedicated largely to livestock production. Ignorance is a factor in dietary deficiencies. People eat certain traditional foods, when the addition of other foods equally available or changes in the methods of preparation and use would provide substantially better nutrition. However, the basic cause of bad diet is poverty. If a construction

worker in Santiago earns by a day's work just enough money
buy two and a quarter pounds of meat, and if he has a family or
eight to feed, meat will obviously not figure on his table. His wife
must settle for cheap starches. Even bread, 22 pounds of which can
be bought for the same day's wages, will be included only spar-
ingly.

Latin Americans are small. This is the first result of the low
amounts of animal protein in their diet, an average of sixteen
grams a day in Brazil and Mexico and of twelve in Peru, which is
a fourth and a fifth respectively of the intake in the United States.
Growth is slow, and the average individual, regardless of age, is
underdeveloped. People age rapidly, presenting the symptoms of
old age in their forties. In Bolivia, where the protein deficit is extreme, children at birth weigh less than normal, and more than a
third of them are notably shorter than the average newborn child.

A study of two groups of boys in Santiago, Chile, revealed that
those who had not gone beyond grade school weighed an average
of 95 pounds at the age of sixteen and were 5 ft. 1 in. tall, while
boys of the same age attending high school weighed 126 pounds
and were 5 ft. 6 in. tall. The difference reflects the diet of the upper and lower classes, though the lower-class group was by no
means at the bottom of the pile, since its members had attended
grade school. Unless a parent is working fairly steadily, he will usually lack the motivation to see that his children attend school, and
probably too they will not have clothes in which to go.

Low protein diets cause other problems. The most common are
dietary dystrophies in children, believed to result from a simulta-
neous shortage of proteins and other nutritive elements. Three out
of every four inhabitants of Lima, Peru, are reported to show the
clinical symptoms of this deficiency.

Many Latin Americans also suffer from a shortage of iron in the
diet, expressing itself in a kind of anemia once blamed on the

tropical climate. Where this deficiency is greatest, the phenomenon of earth-eating is common, a practice which apparently results from a hunger for iron.

The effects of undernourishment are evident in every phase of individual and economic life. They are translated into low worker productivity and high levels of physical and mental illness. The convenient myth that the poor man is happy in his misery has been exploded for what it is. Research among the Indians of the high Andes in the neighborhood of the former Inca capital of Cuzco, for example, has established a level of emotional disturbance fully comparable to that on Madison Avenue.

Low productivity is accompanied by lack of initiative, especially on the part of the rural worker. In addition, the individual condemned to habitual undernourishment will find compensation in substances or liquors which induce a quick if short-lived sense of well-being. This helps to explain a tendency to alcoholism which many rate as the greatest curse of rural Latin America, as well as the persistent use of such drugs as marijuana. Of course, it takes very little alcohol or drug to affect violently a man in low physical condition, so that actual consumption may be much lower than apparent consumption.

Most health problems of Latin America result from diet deficiencies, ignorance of the process of contagion, faulty hygienic practices, contaminated water, and a very unequal distribution of medical facilities as between cities and the country. Malaria, the great scourge of the tropics, has been brought under control almost everywhere by the use of chemical sprays in the past fifteen years, opening up the possibility of development of many areas hitherto unsuited to human living, but tuberculosis, intestinal infections and parasites are still major causes of illness. Eighty per cent of all rural Colombians drink contaminated water, according to the 1960 report of the Health Ministry. More than a million cases of transmissible diseases were recorded in a population of under 15 million people, and 70 per cent of these were of gastro-intestinal origin, mainly diarrheas, enteritis, dysenteries, and typhoid and paratyphoid fevers. Stomach troubles constituted the principal cause of death during the year, while 52 of every hundred persons who died were under two years of age and 33 were under one year.

The story could be paralleled nearly anywhere in Latin America. In all parts, many infants and children die. Infant mortality alone represents 160 per thousand live births in Brazil, 124 in Chile, 81 in Mexico, compared with a rate of 27 in the United States. The accident of geographic location gives the child born in the United States a statistical probability of twenty more years of life than the child born in Latin America.

Perhaps the point at which the gap between actual conditions and minimum human living standards can be most accurately assessed is in relation to housing. Only 20 per cent of the population of Latin America is adequately housed, with another 18 per cent in homes badly needing major repairs, while 62 per cent live in hovels that cannot qualify for description as human habitations. Current construction meets only one-third of the additional needs created by growing population, so that each year more Latin Americans are living in caves like animals.

In Chile, for a population of eight million, the officially calculated shortage of dwelling amounts to half a million, while construction is at an annual rate of 25,000, scarcely enough to take care of the annual population increase without any provision either for normal replacement or for making up the accumulated deficit.

I had recently an opportunity to spend some time in the slums of Lima in the company of American priests who work there. Lima, like other Latin American cities, is growing monstrously because of the high birth rates combined with heavy migration from the country. But economic opportunity and housing are relatively stagnant. Unemployment and underemployment are high. Of the one million Peruvian youths due to enter the work market between 1961 and 1965, scarcely one half can hope to get jobs. And so the slums mushroom. Peru's National Housing Institute estimated in 1962 that only 11 per cent of the population of Peru occupies housing that fulfills minimum requirements of habitability.

No reliable count has been made of the slum-dwellers, but a good round guess for Lima is 400,000. They locate wherever they find a vacant spot, and a major function of the army is the removal of squatters from public and private land. But it has to move fast, because a shanty town springs up in just a few days. The classic example is the *Ciudad de Dios* (City of God). On Christmas Eve 1955, families marched out of Lima and squatted on a series of sand dunes. Like swarming locusts, thousands followed the leaders. The government bowed to a fact, installed water and sewers, and put up some homes.

Mendocita is a different kind of slum, an example of private enterprise. It is a high-class, privately owned slum, where rooms rent for four to five dollars a month. This doesn't seem much until you remember that the head of the house probably gets less than a dollar for a day's work and probably is unemployed more than half the time. Then it adds up to half his month's earnings.

The houses are squat, one-story barracks in long lines, with narrow passageways, built of solid stone and mortar. Rubble is piled high on all sides. There are occasional water faucets on the streets, and a few dwellings along the edge of the jungle have electrical connections from outside.

All kinds of people live in Mendocita. One young fellow I met is a shipping clerk, earning $48 a month. He could afford $16 a month for a room in a good neighborhood, but he prefers to stay with his family and dress well. Another was a television salesman, and believe it or not, he makes some of his sales right in the slum itself, over the gray monotony of which the status-making antennae have begun to sprout. Often they represent an income source, because the enterprising owner can charge neighbors a few cents per session.

But most inhabitants lack education, steady work or prospects. This is a proletariat living on a subhuman level, each fending for himself as best he can. Even family love and affection are squeezed out in the effort to stay alive. The mother's instincts are narrowed to those of the animal which feeds and fights for its young. The teen-ager thinks only of himself. And all is aggravated by the physical pressure of so many humans, ten or twelve to a room, one room squeezed endlessly on top of the next.

Add bad sanitary conditions, no baths, toilets or internal plumbing, the high incidence of tuberculosis, of parasites, and of intestinal disorders, and the crushing heat of the tropics at sea level, and you have Mendocita. The stench is still in my nostrils, the stench of open drains, of rotting refuse, of unwashed bodies, the stench that turned my stomach when I walked just a couple of blocks with Father Mahoney one sunny morning to supervise the distribution of powdered milk supplied by Catholic Relief Services-NCWC from United States surplus food sources.

The physical and moral effects of such living conditions are self-evident. The lack of sanitary facilities, of adequate protection against weather, of minimal comforts, affect health and rest. In such dwellings one can anticipate dirt and promiscuity. A decent family life and proper upbringing of children are impossible. The worker has no inducement to go home. He will prefer to spend his leisure hours elsewhere. The reality of his domestic existence is so bitter that he is tempted to flee from it, to look elsewhere for friendship, understanding and love. These aspects of the life of the poor in Latin America emerge very vividly in the studies of working-class families made in Mexico by Professor Oscar Lewis of the University of Illinois, which are summarized in his fascinating book *Five Families*. It is not surprising that so many families are abandoned by the father. The surprise is that so many are not.

For the wife, who usually does not have this easy way out, the only solution is a stoic submission to her fate. These Latin American peasants are often admirable women, if one can pierce beneath the unattractive appearances, the gnarled hands, the smell of stale perspiration, the ragged clothes, the prematurely old face, the sad eyes. But at this level of existence, there are scarcely enough hours in the day to perform the essential tasks of finding and preparing food, the long daily trips on foot to the market, the tedious preparation of vegetables, the crushing of corn, the collection of firewood, the cooking on primitive stoves. If an hour remains, the tired and sickly body wants to pass it only in aimless leisure. Nor can one expect time to be devoted to religious exercises, especially if they involve participation in a form of activity with no relation to the daily concerns, or require dressing in a way that is entirely out of reach.

For the children, the home is where they eat and sleep piled on top of each other. Two or three share one bed, when there is a bed, without concern for age or sex. The whole family is squeezed into a single room, often sharing it with one or more outsiders, witnesses of the most intimate aspects of the conjugal life of the parents. If they go to church, it is not as a prolongation of the Christian life of their home, but perhaps to get a ticket for a distribution of toys, clothing or food. Many refuse to go because they are ashamed of their bare feet or their rags, or because they have to steal or cheat to survive, and the catechism says that it is a sin to steal.

Such conditions are those neither of a primitive nor of a highly developed society. Grim as they are, they represent a considerably higher living level than that enjoyed by much of Asia and Africa.

It does not, however, follow that they represent a lesser threat, because subjective attitudes and felt needs are as much a part of the situation as are objective conditions, and the Latin Americans have been psychologically integrated into the culture of western Europe, with its stress on material well-being through man's domination of his environment. Today in several Latin American countries a chance spark could set off a reaction as violent and irrational as that which in the African Congo almost precipitated the third World War. People are not willing to wait indefinitely. They know that the civilization of the twentieth century, of which they think of themselves as forming a part, has the capability to provide high levels of material well-being for all its members. Against this background, their own misery can appear only as a gratuitous insult and outrage.

+−+−   *3*

+−+−*New Wine in Old Bottles*

THE BASIC SOCIAL STRUCTURES OF LATIN America, it should now be clear, are a small upper class enjoying wealth and culture, and an inert mass living in ignorance and misery. Neither group is of its nature an instrument of change, the former because it finds things good the way they are, the latter because it lacks the knowledge and power to effect constructive development.

This reality must temper any assessment of the possibility of evolution of Latin American society. As is implicit in what has been said, and as will emerge more clearly, the pressures for change have built up enormously in recent years. But the forces opposing constructive change remain very strong. The class concern of the traditional ruling groups, no matter what the personal views or intentions of individuals, is to maintain the status quo. They will appeal for aid under the pretext that they want to change existing structures, then will use the aid to fortify these structures. North Americans who have taken the protestations at their face value are outraged at the failure of the help (of which they are the principal providers) to effect the declared purposes. Their reaction shows slight political sophistication and less understanding of social realities. The principle of self-preservation is as valid for the class as for the individual. Change must come in spite of, not through the institution to be changed.

The political reality reflects the socio-economic conditions as expressed in structures developed by historical experience. The forms of parliamentary democracy operating within the framework of a written constitution came to all Latin American countries from France, but they were superimposed on the continuing fact of strong-man rule, which itself reflects proximately the conditions of the Conquest and remotely the political systems of the Iberian Peninsula. Few countries enjoy any long period of full political and press freedom, constitutional transfer of power, or free elections with honest counting of ballots.

This is an area in which the North American commentator, particularly at the newspaper level, flounders hopelessly. Deceived by the appearances of parliamentary democracy, he attempts to set up standards based on categories valid within his own experience by which to judge the participation of the people in their government.

The reality is more complex. No replica of United States democracy exists or can exist today in any Latin American country, for the simple reason that none of them possesses the same socio-economic foundations.

For example, the fact of "constitutional government," which is frequently offered as a way to distinguish the "democratic" from the "dictatorial" is a distinction without a difference. A "constitutional government" usually results from elections held under the control of an army junta which had seized power either from a dictator or from a constitutional president, and which manipulated the ballot boxes or otherwise controlled the election process to ensure a majority for its nominees.

Constitutions have little meaning and can always be revised to fit the needs of a given situation. Insofar as they reflect any legal theory, they are based less on political actuality than on French-inspired ideologies of the perfectibility of the human race. They suppose a national intelligence which sees what is good for the country, whereas the fact is that the controlling power during the entire historic period has been a hierarchy of landlords, mineowners, wealthy merchants and churchmen, with a following of lawyers, physicians, army officers and the like. Whenever the theory conflicts with fact, the practical choice is between strong-man rule and anarchy. The dictator, accordingly, has represented the triumph of experience over assumption.

Absence of any vital relationship between constitutional forms and the socio-political structures of the country was vividly illustrated by Brazil's action to meet the crisis when President Janio Quadros resigned suddenly in 1961. Army resistance to the succession of the vice-president, the man next in line for the office, was met by a basic rewriting of the Constitution which transformed the country from a strong-executive system, like that of the United States, to a parliament-dominated executive, like that of Great Britain. Nobody expected the new system to work, because it was totally unrelated to the power realities within the country, and in fact it showed its inadequacy almost immediately. The reduction in the executive power, which was the military's requirement for turning over the government to the new president, left the government less capable of taking urgent social and tax reform measures. A session of Congress summoned for February 1, 1962, was unable for a whole month to muster a quorum. The Brazilians, nevertheless, see nothing ridiculous in their action. The particular situation is more important than the principle, even though it means legislating for exceptions rather than for rules.

Some North American observers, failing to recognize the reasons which make democracy unworkable in Latin America, argue that an element in the Latin American character makes dictatorship the natural form of government. Not a few United States businessmen, finding it easier to make deals with dictators, back this rationalization, as became evident in the nostalgia for Cuba's Batista when the Castro regime produced something quite different from its promise, and such business thinking has on occasion found an echo in the State Department. It will be obvious that I do not share this view. We shall have dictators for so long as one class abrogates to itself the rights of citizenship, and we can anticipate more extreme dictatorships during the inevitable and proximate struggle to alter this socio-political imbalance. The forms that follow the resolution of this struggle may, and I think will, be quite different from our brand of liberal democracy. But there is no reason to anticipate, because of inherent elements in the Latin American character, an ideological dictatorship. The traditional strong man had only the most superficial similarity to the European phenomenon, and as an object of imitation he affected the Latin American scene in just about the same way as have the forms of democracy also imported from Europe.

Having mentioned the State Department, I should add that I do not wish to condemn, out-of-hand, its policy towards Latin American dictators. It has made mistakes, and paid dearly for them, but usually it had no choice other than to recognize and give equal treatment to whatever dictator happened to be in power.

The alternative would be to establish a definition of dictatorship, and under any realistic definition we could never have normal relations with even one-half of our Latin American neighbors.

The division of Latin Americans into Liberals and Conservatives in terms of their traditional party affiliations is no more valid than the division of their governments into dictatorial and democratic, and it is even less excusable for United States observers to be deceived by it since they can see here at home that each of the two political parties, the Republican and the Democratic, is capable of embracing all shades of opinion from the most reactionary to the most advanced.

* Party differences in Latin America were meaningful a century and a half ago, though even then only for the tiny ruling group whose control of the inert masses was so total as to permit the luxury of internal dissension without fear of challenge from a third force. On the one side were ranged the supporters of the established Spanish culture, on the other those of the new ideas blowing from France, iconoclastic, challenging convention, tearing down barriers to progress, but always—be it understood—in the same limited terms in which the barons had sought privileges from King John at Runnymede. The Spanish party understandably sought the support of the Church, conservative by tradition, led by men who owed their privilege to the Spanish Crown, and most of whom were Spaniards by birth. Their opponents shared Voltaire's militant anti-religion, and just as understandably they grouped themselves around the opposing pole of Freemasonry.

In course of time the issues ceased to be significant, and Party allegiances became as much a part of one's conventional position in society as did one's family lines and other appurtenances. Except in a few cases, Conservative parties are little closer to the Church than are Liberal parties, and in any case the new attitudes developing within the Church are rapidly drawing it further away from the ideological position of both political parties. While it may be safe to say that the right wing of the Conservatives is more reactionary than the right wing of the Liberals, it does not follow that the left wing of the former is less advanced than the left wing of the latter. On the contrary, inherent contradictions in the sociopolitical doctrines of the nineteenth century "liberals" have driven their descendants in Latin America, no less than in Europe and the United States, into essentially anti-liberal positions in the field of human rights, preventing them (for example) from accepting the implications of the priority of the rights of parents over those of the state in education.

So unimportant are the shibboleths which divide Conservatives and Liberals, and so deep are the class bonds which bind them, that they have found it expedient and possible to form a long-term coalition in one country. I do not think that they themselves understand the significance of what they have done, and I certainly do not question the honorable intentions of those involved, particularly as the short term aims and results were most desirable.

The country is Colombia, and the facts are as follows. The leaders of Conservatives and Liberals reached an arrangement in August 1957, after a decade of instability and dictatorship, giving each party equal representation and power in all branches of government. All elective bodies consist of an even number of members, one half elected by voters registered as Conservatives and one half elected by voters registered as Liberals. The presidency changes hands each four years, with a Liberal as first president under the agreement. The president gives equal representation in his cabinet to each party, and party equality is also observed in appointing judges, diplomats and other officials.

Alberto Lleras, the man primarily responsible for persuading the warring politicians to accept this sixteen-year truce, took office as president in August 1958, and succeeded in maintaining an uneasy equilibrium for four years. Dr. Lleras, a former secretary general of the Pan American Union, is one of Latin America's most distinguished journalists, and I have known him personally since he presided over a congress of the Inter-American Press Association in Bogotá in 1946. His prestige as a statesman and the personal affection which all Colombians have for him made the political truce work in the negative sense of preventing its dissolution, but they did not make it work in any positive sense of effecting the social transformations which Colombia needs, and which were the alleged justification for suspending the operation of the democratic process.

What has emerged as the continuing reality in the coalition is the protection of the privileged position of the ruling class, Conservative and Liberal alike. The most glaring, though by no means the only example, is the frustration of the land reform project which was to be the great achievement of the coalition, and which I believe Dr. Lleras sincerely believed would result quickly from his acceptance of the presidency. It took more than a year for the government to reach agreement on a project for submission to Congress. The program it proposed was moderate and well thought out. The Catholic hierarchy gave the proposals an enthusiastic blessing, and they can count on wholehearted support from the middle class and from the politically conscious elements in the lower class. In Congress, everyone who favors virtue favors land reform. Nevertheless, it took a further two years to reach agreement on a vague measure, the impact of which will depend entirely on the norms to be adopted by the administering body in applying it. Since Lleras was in 1962 succeeded by a Conservative, it can be assumed that only nominal implementation will occur during the four years of the new President's term of office.

This is the reality of power in Latin America, and baffling as it is to the United States observer, it persists just as obstinately under democratic forms as under open dictatorships. Nor is Colombia by any means the worst offender. Its ways are modern compared, for example, with those of its neighbors to the south, Ecuador and Peru.

The history of land reform in Latin America illustrates the essential nature of this structure, which has historically been based on the ownership of land and which still regards land as the source of wealth, prestige and power. Extensive and drastic land reform has occurred only in three countries: Bolivia, Mexico and Cuba. In all three cases, the transfer of land required a bloody political revolution to break the hold of the landowners over the organs of government before they could be forced, for they would not be persuaded, to permit division of their land. It is, of course, quite proper to question the success of the reforms resulting from these revolutions and I shall discuss this point later. At the moment what I stress is the fact of the resistance.

Understandably enough, there is much pressure for land reform in all countries, and everywhere lip service is paid to the need. The report issued by a conference held under FAO auspices at the end of 1959 shows, however, the limited nature of results. After 26 years of work, Chile's Land Settlement Authority had created fewer than 3,300 units, representing 2.2 per cent of the number of farms in the country. Uruguay, between 1947 and 1959, divided up 2,850 parcels, representing 3 per cent of farms. Guatemala had done rather better since 1955, giving land to 11,700 rural families, or about 3 per cent of all rural families. Venezuela's programs between 1950 and 1959 benefited about 1,600 families. These rates do not begin to take care of the vegetative increase in the population, not to speak of making an impression on the tremendous existing problems of peasants without land. The rhythm of distribution seems to have been stepped up in Venezuela in 1960 and

1961. When President Kennedy visited that country in December 1961, he praised the Betancourt program, saying that it had settled 38,000 Venezuelan families on 800,000 acres. It is, nevertheless, unhappily true of Latin American development plans, as of revolutions to oust dictators, that the long-term fulfilment often falls short of the initial promise. It was stated at the same time that the law looks toward the early resettlement of a total of 300,000 farm families on 76,000,000 acres. Up to now, it has been possible to use land which was in the public domain, land which could be opened up without excessive capital investment because Venezuela had a better highway system than her neighbors, thanks to exploration for and exploitation of oil. Before long, however, it will be necessary to resort to expropriation of big privately-held estates if the program is to proceed as planned. That is when the test will come.

Land distribution to the landless peasants is, however, probably the least of the problems of land reform. The real difficulty is to provide simultaneously to the new farmers the skills and the capital they will need to make their enterprises profitable for themselves and for the national economy. The provision of the skills is part of the vast problem of education, for which no solution is yet visible. The outlook for capital is equally negative. The amounts involved are astronomical. In the United States today, a hundred thousand dollars is a modest investment in a family farm. To find a tenth or even a twentieth of this amount for each of several million farms is beyond the foreseeable ability of Latin America, especially since the demands for investment in industry will be growing rapidly at the same time.

I do not, however, feel any sympathy for another argument frequently adduced against land reform, namely, that family-sized units would be less efficient than the present estates. I do not deny that some crops are suited to big holdings, although development of machines for small farms, especially in Europe and Japan, has narrowed the gap, as has the expansion of such socio-economic devices as the cooperative and the credit union. But the pertinent fact is that any less efficient or less community-oriented enterprise than the typical Latin American estate is unthinkable, and the functional deterioration is progressive. Landlord absenteeism is growing, and with it the gulf between the owner and his workers, so that he neglects even the traditional gifts and favors which formerly represented an important part of their rewards.

A study made by the Economic Commission for Latin America of the United Nations revealed that in 37 per cent of the estates surveyed in the provinces of Santiago and Valparaiso, Chile, the landlord's apathy was a major factor in defective production. In 8 per cent, his lack of interest was the only appreciable barrier to better use of the resources available. Frequently landlords are unwilling to plow back any of the profits. "They do not regard the land as a capital resource in the correct sense of the word," to quote an FAO 1958 report. "They do not expect from it an income representing a proper return on an investment, but rather one which will permit them to live at a certain level. As long as income is adequate for this level, they will not invest in the land in order to raise productivity."

What the upper classes in Latin America will not see is not only that the social system which worked well for them and tolerably for their serfs during two centuries of approximate population balance has no solution for the rapid population rise which now confronts it, but that it is also challenged by the force which long since destroyed it in Europe, namely, a middle class.

Latin America has always had in a limited sense a middle class. Managers are needed to translate the directions of the rulers for the masses, and to supervise the execution of decisions. Nineteenth-century Latin America had such a group of intellectuals, clergy, teachers, artists, and junior army officers. These constituted a class

by themselves, membership in which was determined mainly by
learning and family background. They were closer in outlook to
the upper class than to the urban or rural workers, and they did not
think of themselves as a political power except insofar as they were
a shadow and projection of their respective upper-class masters.

Starting after World War I and at a more rapid tempo since
World War II, however, a new group with different aims and interests has been emerging. It consists of business executives, industry
managers, professionals and intellectuals. Many of its members
came from the upper class, bringing with them its prejudices and
sense of exclusiveness, but many also have risen from the lower
class, toward which their attitudes tend in consequence to be
highly personal, often in a negative way. But their interests are
neither those of the upper nor of the lower class. Their progress
depends on the success of their own class in creating a modern
society, and consequently they must identify with it and strive with
it toward the future. Potentially, they are already stronger than
the upper class, but they have not yet learned to utilize this
strength as a class weapon. And so they war violently among
themselves about means and ends, protagonists of utopias from
St. Thomas More to Mao Tse-tung.

On the fortunes of this new middle class depends the future of
the region. It alone offers a possibility of ordered evolution. The
upper class, no matter what it may pretend, must resist progress. It
has to act according to its interests, and change threatens them.
The lower class lacks the leadership, the internal know-how, to
initiate ordered change. Like the blinded Samson, it has the power
to destroy its enemies with itself, and like him it is prepared to do
so, because life has ceased to be desirable; but that is the limit of its
efforts. Its response is negative, a protest against the wrong it suf-
fers, not a program to remedy that wrong. The new middle class,

on the contrary, does have the know-how and the will to evolve a modern society.

This class has long since taken over in major part the operation of government and of public life from the upper class. Here, however, it is necessary to look carefully beneath the surface to find the more or less hidden manipulators of things, to identify the reality beneath the appearances. This comment is not necessarily cynical. Self-interest is no doubt almost always present in human motivation and action. But by and large, Latin Americans are no more rascally than North Americans or other members of our human race. Politics is the science of the possible, and I think it is enough to say that they excel as politicians. This art is one of the European traditions they have retained, and they practice it with a sophistication and with an enjoyment of the game for its own sake of which Cisneros or Talleyrand would be proud.

From about the time of the First World War, and even earlier in Uruguay, the new middle class, which was then achieving consciousness of itself as a social power, began to see the possibility of utilizing the democratic political structure as an instrument of self-aggrandizement. Previously, the forms of government had simply aped the systems of the United States and France, with a two-party system artificially created out of the two wings of the ruling class, but with the power and the machinery of government remaining entirely within that class.

The change that now took place was that politically ambitious middle-class elements created working arrangements with industrial laboring groups in the cities to help them assert their rights through the instrumentality of the ballot box and thus give a voice in the legislature to this hitherto ignored segment of society. Urban workers were economically depressed and lacked leadership within their own ranks, but they were growing in numbers, and their numbers were what the intellectuals needed to make themselves important.

I do not suggest that there has been no process of democratization taking place throughout Latin America as a result of the creation of this force. On the contrary, I think we are here witnessing a typical social evolution. But I believe that it is important to dwell on the steps in the process and to recognize the limited progress that has yet occurred in most countries. The true as opposed to the apparent base for forward movement remains relatively narrow almost everywhere. The upper class found no great difficulty in accepting the new force as a junior partner, believing it could manipulate it in the same way as it controlled the traditional middle class which preceded it. Besides, it was generally expeditious in the international field, and particularly in dealing with the United States, to create an appearance of a broad-based democratic process. And in addition, it was often possible to agree on parallel short-term aims. Certain aspects of industrial development, for example, especially the processing of agricultural products for local consumption, could be manipulated to the benefit of all parties, the landlord as producer of the primary materials, the middle-class elements as managers and entrepreneurs, and the workers as the industrial labor force. But when the inherently conflicting interest of the middle class as social innovators clashed directly with the social conservatism of the upper class, the latter either prevailed or forced the issue to the point of violent upheaval.

Here, I believe, we have a valid explanation for the see-saw course of politics and the alternation of constitutional government and dictatorship in Latin America during the past thirty or forty years. The dictatorship might represent either the resumption of direct control by an upper class whose power had been challenged by an over-presumptuous middle-class government, or it might— though less frequently—be the instrument of this middle class

organized on a war footing in an all-out challenge to the traditional upper-class monopoly of power. The nominally democratic
government might likewise mean a group truly representative of
the politically active elements in the population (something quite
different from the entire population) but functioning within the
ground rules laid down by the upper class, or it might merely mean
a façade of middle-class elements carried to power through open or
covert manipulation of the electoral process by the upper class.
One of the commonest devices employed by the dictator who has
established his regime firmly is to legalize it by elections, and
American public opinion never fails to be impressed, no matter
how obviously unreal the results. But no matter which of the
above outlined situations exists, the true democratic content is
quite different from what the average North American would con-
clude from a simple comparison of these phenomena with those
of his own political experience.

The successes and failures of the nominally democratic governments of Latin America over the past forty years seem to me the
best demonstration of the validity of the rationalizations I have
presented. These governments have been able to function and
make progress where their aims did not conflict acutely with
those of the old ruling class. Their social legislation is on the whole
far more advanced than in the United States in terms of holidays
with pay, retirement and pension benefits, sickness and maternity
protection, separate allowances and so on. But who are the beneficiaries? Only the industrial workers, who on the one hand must
be kept happy because they are necessary to the middle class, and
who on the other are only a marginal concern to the old upper
class. The great mass of rural workers, the mainstay of the landlord
who is the prototype of Latin American privilege, is excluded from
social legislation. It is true that the benefits to industrial workers
adversely affect important segments of the middle class itself, but

this is the price it has to pay for the alliance it needs. Besides, it can usually pass on the burden without difficulty to the consumer, because of the monopolistic and non-competitive organization of industry and commerce. In addition, social legislation is frequently slanted so as to bear most heavily on the big United States operators in the extractive industries and plantation agriculture, a bias that makes everyone happy, and which the Yankee imperialists somehow manage to live with.

The Latin American industrial worker himself is, of course, quite different from his United States or European counterpart. He is typically a newcomer from the country, and his absorption into urban society is incomplete and precarious. The peasant from the northeast of Brazil, for example, often makes three trips to São Paulo before settling there. The shock from his first contact with the technical environment is such that he returns home in a few days. Even the non-migrant factory worker regards his work as a temporary phase and dreams of going back to the country, if his origins are rural, or of working for himself, if urban. Many have a second and even third spare-time activity, as an emotional step toward the desired independence. After some years of steady employment, they will deliberately slow down in order to be fired and get their separation money, a month's salary for each year's employment. This for them is the capital they need to start up on their own. Managers, for their part, use all possible stratagems to anticipate such moves, the result being highly unstable employment and uneven production rates.

Such inadequate adjustment of workers from the country reflects itself in all areas of life. It is often a factor in the contradictions and surprising electoral alliances which characterize politics. Failing to identify themselves with the world into which they have been transplanted, these workers are interested but passive spectators of public affairs. Even their trades unions they think of as having been created for them, not by them, and they are not conscious members of a class, regarding themselves rather as an inert mass at the bottom of the heap. They maintain the values and traditions of their rural homes, or adapt them in unexpected ways. Thus, in the cities of Brazil, sects such as Xango teem in the shadows of the skyscrapers. The slums are full of pharmacies selling syrups, drugs and vitamins, but nobody bothers to buy vegetables. And families with radio and television have not learned to filter the polluted water they drink.

The dynamic growth of new industries is impressive, but not less striking is the widespread lack of organization, the plethora of personnel not productively employed, the abuse of overtime, the high manufacturing costs under protection, the lack of planning for industrial investment, especially the inadequacy of electricity which results in constant interruptions of industrial production, the cult of low wages and high profits. Brazil's labor minister told me in early 1962 of an industrial enterprise in which five directors had paid themselves the equivalent of the wages of 850 employees in 1961. Meanwhile, the wealthy put their profits in foreign banks, complain constantly of the poor quality of domestic products and buy expensive foreign goods, thereby maintaining the smuggling apparatus which in not a few countries is the most dynamic, most profitable and most corrupt business.

Efforts to eliminate by available constitutional means the privileges of the upper class have all ended in failure or continuing stalemate. I have already briefly summarized the lack of progress of all such constitutional efforts at land reform, admittedly the first step toward a modernization of Latin America's economy. Tax reforms designed to diminish the maldistribution of wealth and to discourage antisocial uses of wealth, such as hoarding large extensions of land without using it, as a hedge against inflation and in anticipation of increase in value, have always foundered on the same rock. Guatemala under Arbenz offered a striking example. His extremely left-wing and Communist-sympathizing government introduced sweeping reforms on paper, and its dictatorial powers enabled it to make considerable progress in dividing land among the peasants. Yet it never felt strong enough to tackle the tax structure, not even to introduce a progressive income tax.

The strength of Peronism in Argentina was and is its identification with the interests of the middle class and labor, both of which are much stronger there than in most Latin American countries. The urban population constitutes well over 60 per cent of the total, and the number of persons employed by manufacturing industry is as high as the number in agriculture. Nevertheless, the basis of the economy is still a colonial-type exportation of agricultural products (meat and wheat), the raising and movement of which remains in the hands of a small upper class.

Perón was able to inflict deep wounds on this class, but only at the cost of inflicting them also on the national economy, which he did not succeed in transforming quickly enough to compensate for the fall in traditional exports. Before he could swing the balance of power decisively to the other side, he was defeated by the inherent defect in dictatorship, the total corruption that grows from total power. He lost his sense of proportion, so that wealth and power became his goals, and tyranny his means. His overthrow restored the control of the traditionalists in an extremely unstable equilibrium with middle-class Liberals. Only by the effective disfranchisement of an admitted majority of Argentines, because elections with no holds barred would produce a Peronist majority, has the regime survived.

The old upper class can never hope to regain its full control, for it seems to be inherent in the evolution we are witnessing throughout the world that social change today can move only in one direction. Progress can be restrained but can never be reversed. But it remains to be seen whether even such obvious facts as those on the record in Argentina can persuade people to adjust themselves to a reality they find distasteful.

Colombia during the 1950's went through a very curious dictatorial experience, which some commentators liken to that of Perón in Argentina. In the late 1940's, a Liberal politician named Gaitan rose to great prominence on a program which promised to depart from the traditional positions of the two political parties and strive for basic social change. His assassination on a Bogotá street, in April 1948, produced a violent popular reaction almost without parallel in Latin American history. For several days, mobs swept the city in a senseless outburst of pillage, looting and burning, giving the Spanish language a new word, a *bogotazo*. From the capital, the riots spread across the country, causing damage estimated by the United States Embassy at $570,000,000.

The army restored public order, and the government sought to calm the populace by a number of decrees designed to improve the living conditions of the masses, including a very significant one aimed at land distribution which declared that in the present circumstances it was necessary "to bring about social stability by means of augmenting the number of proprietors."

The phrase *in the present circumstances* was, of course, intended to stress for the upper class the inevitability of sacrifice. But they refused to listen, and soon they were forcing the government once more into a policy of repression instead of conciliation, a trend which culminated with the installation as president of arch-Conservative Laureano Gomez, the head of a determined counter-revolutionary force, and his unseating by the army to initiate the dictatorship of General Gustavo Rojas Pinilla, after some 100,000 lives had been sacrificed to partisan passion and madness. Since

Colombia's population is about a twelfth that of the United States, the slaughter was equivalent to the killing of more than a million people in this country.

Rojas Pinilla tried to do some of the same things in Colombia that Perón had done in Argentina. From the outset, he found himself in total opposition to the two traditional parties, who closed ranks against him and treated him as being in fact the enemy of the existing order which he proclaimed himself to be. Like Perón, he sought to establish a broad base of support among the industrial masses and even to create a movement paralleling the *descamisados*, the shirtless ones. But Colombia is much less industrially developed than Argentina, and the forces of conservatism are much stronger and more socially cohesive. Rojas Pinilla was soon driven to excesses of tyranny in order to cling a little longer to power. He succeeded in turning the Church against him as well as the politicians, and in consequence he lost support so rapidly that it proved possible to oust him in a bloodless coup and to transfer power to the coalition of Conservatives and Liberals described earlier.

I have said that no examples exist in Latin America of a transition within the constitutional and democratic framework from the semi-feudal static society to a modern dynamic one. We do, however, have three examples of major social change produced by revolutionary violence, and it is interesting to look at these and assess the significance of the results. The three countries in question are Mexico, Bolivia and Cuba.

+ − + −   *4*

+ − + − *Successful Social*
Revolution—Mexico

AN EVENT STILL CHARGED WITH EMO-
tion, the Mexican revolution began as a political reaction against
tyrannical dictatorship in 1910 and quickly assumed social and ideological content. Fierce civil wars from 1910 to 1917 almost completely annihilated the old upper class. The Church, which had
allowed itself to become emotionally and politically associated with
the upper class and which was a part of that class as the owner of
great estates, became a major target of the revolution, and the
struggle continued into the 1930's, with bitter and violent persecution under Calles. Marxism assumed the ideological role Freemasonry had played for the anticlerical party in the previous cen-

tury, bringing Mexico under strong left-wing influences. These continue to hold official favor, though today as shibboleths rather than policy guides.

Basic institutional changes were carried out during the thirty years between 1910 and 1940, the semi-feudal agrarian economy being transformed by breaking up large landholdings, distributing land to peasants, establishing communal villages or *ejidos* (a form of landholding and exploitation which was a deliberate throwback to Indian customs), reducing foreign participation in and control over the economy, emancipating the Indians, and extending public education.

The reaction of United States public opinion was particularly negative during the 1930's, when President Lázaro Cárdenas nationalized land, railroads and the foreign-owned petroleum industry. The Mexican economy, nevertheless, survived, and the need for allies in World War II hastened and smoothed the process of international acceptance of the *fait accompli.*

The Mexicans, for their part, showed remarkable maturity by reversing the direction of the revolution as soon as it had achieved the social aims they sought. Since 1940, they have withdrawn steadily from the alliance with the ideological left on which they had leaned while engaged in destroying the old right-wing social structures. Accordingly, the slogans of the class struggle have given way increasingly to appeals for harmony and balance, and national efforts have been more and more concentrated on developing the productive capacities of the country to provide material and social benefits for the citizens.

Politically, the Mexican revolution has created a distinctive system of control of the machinery of government. A single party called the Party of Revolutionary Institutions has been forged out of all elements in the country other than the Church and big business, and such is the cohesion and community of interest of all

these other elements—agrarian, labor, bureaucratic and business—
that the coalition is perfectly stable and can function within the
framework of democratic elections without any danger of losing
control.

The technique has some similarities to the coalition more recently established in Colombia, except that in the Colombian coalition the two parties retain their identity and are guaranteed
absolutely equal shares of power, at least in as far as mathematics
can accomplish that division, while in Mexico the various interests
form a single composite and lack individual political organs. Another difference is that the Mexican arrangement has ensured a
powerful executive, able to apply a logical and strong policy of national development, while the Colombian has up to now hamstrung the executive and failed to provide the inspired leadership
of which the first president under the party truce was undoubtedly
capable. Perhaps this difference is inherent in the nature of the
function entrusted by the coalition to the executive in the two
cases, for power in Colombia resides in a conservative oligarchy,
whereas in Mexico it has been seized by the innovators who want
and need change and modernization.

Another distinction of the Mexican system is that it has for many
years solved one of the toughest problems of Latin American
politics: the transfer of power from regime to regime. It is true that
this transfer has taken place only within the ranks of the party and
allows each president a big voice in choosing his successor. But at
least the tradition of the dictator has been broken, and I think it
would be quite difficult for a future Mexican president to convert
himself into a *caudillo*.

There is still little sign of the emergence either of a two-party
system as in the United States, or of a multi-party system permitting various socio-economic groups in turn to exercise legislative
and executive authority either singly or in changing coalitions, as

in France, and one might argue that all that has been effected is
the substitution of one ruling class by another. In a sense, this is
true. Yet I also think that the new class is not only more broadly
based than the old, but that its intrinsic logic and philosophy are
carrying it toward a more democratic system. What this requires is
the triumph of a national over a class consciousness, both on the
part of the dominant elements constituting the government and
on the part of the elements now excluded from participation in
public life, namely, the Church and the old upper class. Such a
change of attitudes has to overcome deep emotional obstacles,
but once a new power balance is recognized as an irreversible fact,
the rest is a matter of time.

What benefits has the revolution brought to Mexico? To begin
with for land reform, one of the early rallying cries, the statistics
are impressive, especially when contrasted with the minimal progress made in countries in which the old upper class remains in
power. From the proclamation of the new constitution in 1917 to
the election of Cárdenas as president in 1934, some seventeen million acres were distributed. Cárdenas initiated a new and intense
phase of the revolution based on class struggle and without too
much regard for economic consequences. During his six years of
office, he added approximately another twenty million acres. Although the revolution settled down in the subsequent period, the
tempo of land distribution has scarcely slackened, so that the total
acreage affected rose to more than a hundred million in 1958, and a
further twelve million in the following three years, to produce a
figure of 116 million acres at the start of 1962. President López
Mateos, who took office in 1958, plans to maintain the same rate
of nearly 350,000 acres monthly during the next three years. This
is almost half as much each month as the entire Venezuelan distribution during the two years of the Betancourt program singled

out for praise by President Kennedy on his December 1961 trip to Venezuela.

The effects of the land distribution are harder to assess. One of the most illogical things about the Mexican revolution is the Indian myth it has evolved. Otherwise perfectly rational spokesmen will declaim with wild-eyed enthusiasm about the determination of the movement to restore the Indian civilization and undo the effects of the Conquest. The violence to history and fact required to torture this fiction into any kind of a working theory can find parallels only in George Orwell's fancy. In the common understanding of Mexicans as of all Latin Americans, an Indian is one who speaks an Indian language and lives outside the European culture brought by the Spaniards. The new Mexico is trying very hard to teach its Indians a European language (Spanish) and culture and thereby to transform them from Indians to Mexicans. There has been a steady decrease since the revolution in the percentage of those who speak only an Indian dialect, and today it is probably not more than 10 per cent of the population. At the present rate of transition, few in Mexico will speak only an Indian tongue by the end of the century.

All this is good. What is, to say the least, confusing to the observer is to have it presented as a restoration of Indian civilization and an undoing of the Conquest. All Latin Americans tend to be schizophrenic about their Spanish heritage, and this emotional disturbance is particularly in evidence in the Mexican revolution in so far as it continues to present the Indian as a symbol of oppression and proclaims his redemption as a major aim. Today, most Mexicans sentimentally identify their nation with the Indian rather than with the Spanish heritage, while in actual fact treating the Indian as the lowest element in society and seeking to place themselves socially as far away from their own Indian background as possible. So deep rooted is the sentimental conditioning, that Mexican psychiatrists have developed their own local applications of Freud, interpreting the Indian mother as the loved symbol of maternity and the Spanish-colonial woman as cold and rejecting, and presenting the Spanish soldier of the Conquest as the father figure whose absence has developed in Mexicans a hostility to Spaniards and by extension to all foreigners. Even a slight acquaintance with the historical acceptance by the Spaniards, including those of the highest standing, of Indian women as legal wives, reveals the absurdity of this theory. Such acquaintance with history, however, is totally absent. The revolution has nowhere been more successful than in creating a myth divorced from all reality, and this may one day prove a serious weakness in the midst of its undoubted successes.

The Indian myth underlay a major false step taken by the revolution in the early years of land reform, an error which perhaps came the more naturally because Communist theoreticians in high places interpreted the action as a move in their direction. The big estates were handed over to the peasants under an adaptation of an old Indian system of communal land use known as the *ejido*. The transfer brought political and social satisfactions but also rural economic chaos coupled with lowering of agricultural production and a deterioration in the fertility of the land.

The new ruling class, however, when faced with the dilemma, showed a flexibility more typical of the United States than of the Latin character (Mexico is, after all, our nearest neighbor and the most culturally influenced), and a modified but workable system of distribution has been evolved, with the result that land tenure today is about equally divided between families on communal holdings and those on small to medium-sized privately owned farms.

Most countries seeking (as Mexico is) to modernize an underdeveloped economy tend to devote their principal efforts to industry. Even if land reform is a proclaimed goal, they will be satisfied with land distribution and leave it to the new owner to find his own ways of improving his techniques. Mexico early decided to apply modern methods in all sectors of the economy—agriculture, industry and commerce—and to keep all three elements in step. Accordingly, it has undertaken enormous outlays for developmental activity to provide the infrastructure of transportation, power, irrigation works, agricultural and industrial credit, and the like. This policy, combined with massive land reclamation programs to add to the total area of land in productive use, has steadily raised the level of agricultural output, so that today the country supplies domestic food needs and leaves a considerable surplus for export. The share of agriculture in total commodity exports has been rising steadily and represented half of the total in 1960. Interestingly enough, in the light of what was said above, the improvement in agricultural production is concentrated in the individually owned farms. The Indians in their *ejidos* have been bypassed, and they continue to specialize in the production of corn and beans by traditional primitive methods, with the result that the gap between them and the so-called mestizos is growing wider.

Between 1945 and 1957, agricultural output more than doubled, while population increased by 40 per cent. Although agriculture still occupies more Mexicans than all other activities combined, it has kept its share of the gross national product with a declining proportion of the labor force. In twenty years the country has gone a long way towards changing from a predominantly subsistence economy in agriculture to a market economy. This was done by bringing new land under cultivation, by expanding irrigation (to 7.4 million acres in 1962), using more fertilizer, better seeds, more machines, and by concentrating these improvements on big holdings, as just noted, again an imitation of the United States approach.

Progress in industry has been even more substantial, with an increase of 130 per cent in the volume of industrial production between 1939 and 1957. The principal advances resulted from the more efficient use of existing plants and the addition of new facilities in such established industries as iron and steel, cement, chemicals, paper, sugar and glass, but many new industries have been added in the fields of chemicals, aluminum, auto assembly, and others. The oil industry suffered severely after nationalization but has recovered steadily if not spectacularly, so that production is double what it was in the late 1930's. The oil budget in 1961 was three-quarters that of the federal government. The rate of growth in heavy industry suggests that Mexico is on its way to becoming an industrial nation. In spite of a general slackening of the rhythm of progress in all Latin America in the late 1950's together with a decline in demand for primary commodities, the Mexican economy continued an impressive growth rate. The real output of goods and services, for example, increased 5.7 per cent in 1960 over the previous year. The federal debt, two-thirds internal, is equal to roughly one year's federal expenditures.

The facts and figures cited show that Mexico has made notable advances in recent years, moving incidentally at a rate not equaled by any other Latin American country. They indicate that the lower classes, whose plight provided the rationale for the revolution, have won specific advantages, and that to the new status of the Indian resulting from the community's awareness of his existence is coupled a greater possibility for the individual in the lowest classes to improve his condition by his own efforts. Such mobility, both social and geographic, is in fact basic to all advance, for it reflects the transfer from peonage to personal freedom, from a chattel to a human level. The process has been accompanied by increasing government participation in industry, its share representing 40 per cent by 1962.

Mexico, nevertheless, still has far to go. There certainly is no indication of movement toward a one-class society, even if a one-
party government has been established in the political sphere. On
the contrary, the distribution of the new national wealth has been
extremely uneven, weighted heavily in favor of the owners of
capital and generally of the upper income groups. The Economic
Commission for Latin America, for example, reported in 1954 that
between 1939 and 1952, wages, salaries and incomes of small
entrepreneurs increased at an annual rate of 4.4 per cent, while
profits, interests and rent rose 10.1 per cent. A little earlier, the
International Bank for Reconstruction and Development had
noted a big increase, to over 40 per cent of the total, in the share of
the national income going to profits, and a corresponding fall to
less than 24 per cent of the total in the share going to wages and
salaries. A chronic inflation which squeezes the real income of the
poor, and which continues to a greater or lesser extent in almost
every Latin American country, is a big factor in that situation.

As has been indicated, the Indians who got land under the *ejido*
system have been left very much to their own devices in the use to
which they put it. Because of a greater social flexibility, some individuals are making and benefiting from improvements, but as a
class the *ejido* farmers still live on or below the subsistence level,
although there are indications of some gains, such as a rise in the
percentage of the population which wears shoes and eats wheat
bread. A rise in the percentage has, however, to be kept in perspective. Out of a population of 34,625,000 at the 1960 census, an estimated twenty million Mexicans still buy no shoes, no processed
soap, no clothing, no processed food. They live on what they can
raise and barter. Some 35 per cent of Mexicans buy 70 per cent of
all shaving creams and cosmetics, 65 per cent of all soft drinks,
and 95 per cent of all automobiles.

Where progress is most evident is naturally in the cities. Even in the slums, radios have become so common as no longer to distinguish the income level of the owner, which can be measured more accurately by the presence or absence of a gas stove, a television set, and knives and forks.

The selection of indices illustrates a normal part of socioeconomic progress. People coming into enjoyment of a pre-existing civilization do not rate its benefits in the same order as those who inherited them. Most of us would think knives and forks on the table far more basic than a radio, yet among lower-class urban families in Mexico, the incidence of the latter is much higher. Five families out of ten use knives and forks; eight have radios. And housing is still more backward. The rising population compounded by the drift to the cities is probably increasing an already intolerable crowding in slum conditions. Nearly half of all family dwellings in Mexico City, the third most populous city in the hemisphere after New York and Buenos Aires, have only one room, and nearly another quarter have only two rooms. More than half the families in the city lack running water in their homes. These are official figures published in 1954 and referring to a count made in 1950. Today, the situation is probably worse, because in the interval the population has been growing faster than housing or services.

With these developments has come a substantial change in the nature and complexion of the social classes in Mexico. If we go back to the end of the last century, we find more than 90 per cent of the population in the lower class, with nine-tenths of this class composed of landless agricultural workers (peons) and one-tenth urban. The creation of the *ejidos* made a big dent. Nearly a fourth of the entire population became *ejido* farmers, and considerable numbers of these have entered or are in the process of entering the middle class. During the past quarter century the urban proportion of the lower class has grown, so that today the lower class constitutes about 80 per cent of the population, and one member in four lives in a city. Since the revolution has always stressed the class content of its gospel, industrial workers in urban centers tend to be strongly class conscious. It is remarkable, nevertheless, that only a small proportion of Mexicans are members of trades unions. As in Latin America generally, trades union membership figures are no more reliable than other statistics and, for reasons to be discussed later, labor organizations serve political or personal purposes rather than the economic ends of the working class for which they exist in the United States.

The old upper class and its subordinate middle class, which together constituted a tenth of the Mexican population at the end of the century, have both disappeared. I do not mean that every member has been annihilated physically, although a considerable number were during the civil wars. But they have become submerged in new classes.

The new upper class consists of bankers, industrialists and big businessmen. Ironically enough, the foreign companies which won concessions in pre-revolution Mexico were the instigators of the change which laid the foundations of this class. The technicians, managers, scientists and professionals trained by them became the leaders of the revolution, then government ministers and generals when the revolution triumphed, and they finally used their power to build their own personal empires. This is consequently a non-aristocratic group, dedicated to social change and economic growth. It is small in numbers, perhaps one per cent of the population, but individual incomes run very high.

The most rapid growth has been in the new middle class, which is assuming the characteristics of the middle class of developed countries, though its proportion in the population remains small. It comprises government officials, teachers, small businessmen, storekeepers, skilled workers, small industrialists, intellectuals, professionals, small private landowners, and some *ejidatarios*. This grouping covers a wide range of income, living standards, living habits and attitudes. As yet, it does not have too much awareness of the common interests that cut it off from the other classes, and indeed to a considerable extent it is a projection and affiliate of the new upper class. However, there is every reason to suppose that it will continue its development towards full middle-class status.

Evolution of attitudes toward the United States, and particularly toward investment from this country, is particularly interesting in the light of the anti-Americanism which was a favorite theme of the revolution in its first phase. Nationalization of oil in the 1930's, a policy which affected British interests more than American, brought such outraged protests from the representatives of big business everywhere as to seem to guarantee the absence of United States investors from the Mexican scene for the foreseeable future.

Much anti-American sentiment remains, and it is logical to anticipate a vocal continuance of the resistance to a cultural invasion which is bound to irritate Mexicans for as long as the United States is notably more highly developed and bigger than Mexico. Given these conditions, which are likely to continue, plus geographic contiguity, cultural penetration is inevitable, and so is resistance to it.

What is surprising is to find that below the conscious level of stylized protest there resides a deep sense of friendship and identification of interest. The facts seem again to be triumphing over the theories. And the facts are impressive. A major source of income for Mexico is the work of the *braceros*. More than a million and a half of these unskilled Mexican farmhands have worked at some time north of the border. The wages were low and the living conditions horrible, but for most of them, these were the highest wages and the best work conditions they ever knew. They remember the United States as the place where they earned enough to buy a radio, add a separate bedroom to their one-room shack, perhaps to buy a plot of land.

Many more millions of Mexicans have met one or other of the more than 500,000 vacationers who trip south annually across the border and fan out over the country to every remotest shrine and ruin. They constitute a cross section of the people of the United States—vulgar, loudmouthed, boastful, contemptuous of foreigners, especially *spiks*, but also open, generous, naively anxious to help, craving esteem, totally without class consciousness. They leave behind them not only precious cash but a balance of good will, reflected—for example—in the attitudes of school children, a sampling of whose opinions has revealed that a big majority rank the United States first among all foreign countries in their affection, and that a surprisingly big proportion would like to be United States citizens. The existence of such a secret ambition is perhaps not surprising. What is noteworthy is a readiness to admit its presence.

Not less noteworthy is the upsurge of United States investment in recent years, coupled with a big invasion of businessmen from this country, fifteen thousand of whom make their home in Mexico because they like the climate, the tempo of life, the low cost of living and the opportunities to make profits. United States advertisers and their techniques are everywhere visible; the same companies push the same razor blades, automobiles, soft drinks and tooth paste under the same trade names. The television programs, commercials and filler alike, are translations or superficially adjusted adaptations of our own.

When the Mexican revolution began in 1910, United States direct investment in Mexico was approaching a half billion dollars. Great Britain was then the biggest outside investor, but we soon outstripped her, and by 1924 had increased our private investments, three-quarters of the total direct, to over a billion. During the 1930's, a sharp drop occurred because of depression and nationalization, so that United States direct investment went below half a billion in 1936 and near a quarter billion in 1939. The nature of the investments, however, remained very much the same during all this period, namely, mining, transportation and public utilities. There was a big stake in oil until nationalization.

Since World War II, United States direct investment has again grown rapidly, but with very different characteristics. The Mexican government and public opinion remain extremely sensitive to foreign control of any segment of the economy where such control might tend to slow down or divert national development policy. Accordingly, the trend begun in the 1930's continues to restrict foreign capital in such areas, including petroleum production and public utilities. Transfer of control today, however, is effected not by expropriation but by stock purchase, which may be made either by the government or by Mexican capitalists, according to circumstances. The substantial steel industry is now wholly in Mexican hands, as is the electric power industry formerly owned by United States and Canadian interests. The last private producer of electricity in the country, a Canadian-controlled corporation, was bought out by the government during 1961. There is, however, no pressure to nationalize the telephone monopoly, in which more than half the capital is Mexican.

In line with this policy and climate, new United States capital has moved into manufacturing and trade, so that more than half the total is in this field. While participation is spread among many companies, the bulk of the new capital is in United States-owned or -controlled subsidiaries of giant domestic corporations, such as General Motors, General Electric, DuPont, Sears Roebuck and Woolworth. Not a few Mexican businessmen feel that it is difficult if not impossible to compete with companies which have the financial backing, the immense research facilities, market know-how and benefit of internationally promoted trade marks, and there is constant criticism that United States firms tend to monopolize any area into which they enter, to favor United States sources of supply, and to siphon profits out of the country.

While the debate continues, so does the flow of United States capital into the Mexican economy. By 1957, United States direct investments were well above the high figure of $735 million reached in 1924, and subsequent years have continued the climb. Most of the $125 million foreign capital investment in Mexico during 1961 originated in the United States. During that year, United States corporations and their affiliates furnished 7 to 8 per cent of Mexico's gross national product, and paid nearly 20 per cent of all corporation taxes.

Regarding the debated level of profits, some general guideposts to the extent of profits taken out of the country exist. A United Nations report on foreign investments reached a figure of 21.8 per cent as the average annual earnings on private investment in Latin America as a whole for the year 1951. A considerably lower but still substantial rate of earnings is presented for Mexico in figures published by the United States Department of Commerce for a six-year period from 1950 through 1955. These show profits of about 10 per cent annually on a half billion dollars invested there, of which 4 per cent was plowed back and 6 per cent removed from the country in the form of profits. Earnings in 1956 were nearly 12 per cent, of which over 7 per cent was reinvested and less than 5 withdrawn, but in 1957, when the profits fell below 10 per cent, somewhat more than half was withdrawn and only 4.6 per cent reinvested.

Substantial as are these profit rates, they are certainly no higher and probably considerably lower than those earned by local capital which even with the revolution has not entirely shed the traditional Latin American business attitude of small volume and high gains. No doubt an important reason for government satisfaction with continuing and even expanding participation of foreign capital in non-sensitive areas is that it pressures local enterprise to modernize operations and attitudes. Sears Roebuck, for example, has had a tremendous impact on retail trade in Mexico City, as in other big cities of Latin America, by establishing such concepts as big turnover for a mass buying public, and it has also helped light industry by creating the needed demand for small consumer items which can be produced cheaply only in quantity.

No area of the Mexican revolution is less subject to logical analysis than its relations with the Catholic Church. In the broadest terms, the emotional situation in the early part of the century was at least as much to blame as were objective differences of interest and purpose between the Church in Mexico and the revolution. As the influence of Marxism grew during the period when the revolutionaries were looking for ways to whip up a mystique, the Church became the symbol of all that was holding Mexico back from the modern world. The anti-Catholic and anti-religious propaganda was handled with consummate skill by the theoreticians of the movement, its best known and most effective expression being the crudely propagandistic murals of Orozco, Rivera and Siqueiros, who prostituted their art and falsified the historic facts in the service of a partisan cause more shamelessly than any of the talents enslaved by Hollywood or Madison Avenue. Not satisfied with simply making paintings of Indians, they set out to pervert all the established principles of decency, presenting Justice as a debauched drunk and God the Father surrounded by harpies instead of angels. Bishops, priests and friars appeared as obscene vultures fattening throughout the course of Mexican history on the downtrodden Mexican masses, who had to await the arrival of their

Marxist liberators to achieve their historic destiny in political, social and economic terms.

This was how Mexico reached the strange situation of a country with a total commitment to the Catholic Church as a religion and an equally total commitment to the destruction of the Catholic Church as an institution. Only a very small group formally rejected the Church, and even many of the followers and active helpers in the bitter persecution which destroyed churches and killed or exiled the Catholic leaders remained in their own minds loyal Catholics. So deep rooted in Mexico is the concept of membership of the Church that one of the elements marking transition from a state of Indian tribalism to full participation as a Mexican in the national life is joining the Catholic Church. Accordingly, even during the anti-religious phase of the revolution, it was making converts to Catholicism of all the Indians whom it succeeded by its social action in lifting on the socio-economic scale from barbarism to the fringes of civilized life.

This was not by any means the first assault on the Church in Mexico. On the contrary, it had never enjoyed any long period of normality since the beginning of the nineteenth century. Because of Spanish opposition and internal unrest, formal relations between the Holy See and an independent Mexico were not resumed until 1836, although five years earlier six bishops had been named through intermediaries, after the hierarchy had dwindled to a single bishop.

In the middle of the nineteenth century, relations between Church and State got steadily worse. The 1857 constitution withdrew recognition of Catholicism as the state religion, and four years later the separation of the two powers was declared. During the 1870's, a series of anticlerical laws nationalized Church property, introduced civil marriage, and expelled a number of religious orders. The long dictatorship of Porfirio Diaz, from 1876 to 1911, continued the same general policy, though in his later years the dictator applied the anticlerical laws less rigorously.

The 1917 constitution introduced by the successful revolution and still in force merely carried this trend a step further. It decreed compulsory secular education, which in line with the attitudes toward the Church laid down by the theoreticians of the movement is positivist, materialist and anti-religious, forbade acts of worship outside the church buildings, denied the Church the right to hold property, even the church buildings (owned but not maintained by the state). It is today illegal for a priest to appear on the street in clerical dress. Nuns are not only forbidden to wear their habits but to live in community. Religious teaching bodies are forbidden to engage in any way in primary or secondary instruction, in the training of teachers, or in any kind of educational activities for workers or peasants.

The firm establishment of the revolution during the 1930's was accompanied by a gradual relaxation of the anti-religious measures, and since about 1940 an unwritten agreement has operated to permit the Church to function fairly normally in the spiritual sphere, so that it has in fact regained much of the influence it formerly enjoyed. The constitutional provisions have not been revoked. The state still claims total authority in the religious sphere. It would be legally possible for a president to try to promote a schismatic church, as President Calles did when he set up a "married" priest with the title of patriarch in one of the churches of Mexico. The Church continues to lack legal status. Many amazing provisions enliven the statute books, such as the laws of several states fixing the number of priests authorized to serve within the state (Yucatan permitted forty, provided they solemnly affirmed that they did not keep holy water in the churches but baptized with running water), or those requiring that a bishop be a married man, as was specified by Tabasco. But the general tenor of the enforcement has been steadily relaxed, and a president of Mexico is again able to state publicly, if not that he is a Catholic, at least that he is a believer, which in the ears of the listener means exactly the same thing.

Schools under Church auspices function openly at the primary and secondary levels. Activities in the publishing field are both many and professionally organized. I was most favorably impressed by the business planning and technical levels of a printing plant operated in Mexico City by the La Salle Brothers as a combined center of Catholic publishing and vocational training for young men. The Jesuits also have a modern publishing center, with good printing facilities, in Mexico City, issuing a broad spectrum of publications which include a weekly newspaper, general and specialized monthlies, and a range of pamphlets.

The restoration of the Catholic clergy is a remarkable chapter in which United States Catholics played a big part by building and maintaining a seminary in New Mexico to train candidates for the priesthood at a time when all the seminaries in Mexico were closed. The number of priests in the country fell to an estimated 500 in 1935, and for a long time all but six of the bishops were in exile, while the priests and bishops who stayed were in hiding. For three years, from 1926 to 1929, religious ceremonies in the churches were suspended by order of the bishops, with the approval of the Holy See, because services could be continued only by observing civil laws which would have transformed the nature of the Church and converted it into a national schismatic sect. Today, by contrast, there are nearly 6,000 priests, almost twice as many as a century ago, and nearly 2,000 seminarists. Sisters number more than 18,000, and nearly half a million children attend Catholic schools. Indeed, it is worthy of note that Mexico sends missionaries to other countries, Jesuits to Japan, and Holy Ghost Fathers to

Peru, and that a foreign missions seminary has functioned since 1948.

Devotion to the Blessed Virgin has always been a characteristic of Catholicism in Latin America, a devotion expressed particularly in Mexico at the shrine of Our Lady of Guadalupe. Even at the height of the persecution, the enemies of religion never dared interfere with the services at the basilica of Guadalupe, which became more than ever a symbol of the permanence and national character of Mexican Catholicism. Since World War II, public expression of Catholic opinion in the religious and allied social fields has increased steadily. What is particularly noticeable is that many of the organized groups which come continually in pilgrimage to Guadalupe represent elements in society which grew out of and reflect the revolution: trades unions, housing settlements, *ejidos*. Yet among the masses, and particularly in the ranks of the important group whom I may call the sub-intellectuals (young people in white-collar jobs who have only high schooling but think of themselves as educated in a society in which illiteracy is still normal), there exists alongside religious devotion a deep ambivalence of attitude. They have been conditioned by their education to regard the Catholic Church as the historic enemy of the Mexican people, and it is as unthinkable for them to question this official version as it would be for the average North American to challenge the established role of Washington or Lincoln in this country's national evolution.

The change in relations that I have been describing has, as is obvious, taken place on both sides. As the development of events altered the objective realities of the relationship between the two powers, the attitudes of each have also altered. In a sense, the revolution has been the victor in the contest, for it has ended the traditional Latin American concept under which the Church ruled while the state governed. The state has become the undisputed ruler. On the other hand, the Church has also won an important victory, the only one that should count for her. It has established, and indeed confirmed in the blood of martyrs, the unshakable solidity of the religious faith of the Mexican people. To destroy that faith was an avowed purpose of the revolution, but since its leaders had the good sense—in spite of their personal prejudices—to recognize that this aim was not essential to the success of their purpose, they have been able to accept defeat with some grace and to begin to make the practical adjustments that must flow from such recognition.

There is, accordingly, reason to anticipate the gradual development of a new and stable equilibrium of the two powers in Mexico, which is most likely to result from movement toward a juridic arrangement similar to that which exists in the United States. What seems to me the greatest danger lies in the development of a political opposition in Mexico. I do not mean that the development of an opposition as such is undesirable; on the contrary, it is a logical next step in a country which is laying the basis for a democratic regime. The danger lies in the fact that the only opposition with any real potential on the horizon is the National Action Party, a party of Christian inspiration, something like the Christian parties that have loomed so large in the postwar life of Western Europe.

This of course is the logical ideological position for a mass party in Mexico, in the light of the total Christian emotional dedication of the people. But the historical experience is such that both supporters and enemies inevitably think of this party as a revival of the Church's claims to rule in the temporal order. And herein lies the danger, a danger that might erupt into new persecution and civil disorder, because the National Action Party could easily reach a position of being able to challenge the present single party at the polls. In Mexico City, between 1946 and 1955, it doubled its strength, from 16.2 to 32.7 per cent of the total votes cast. And Mexico City contains some 13 per cent of the country's population and its most educated and politically sophisticated citizens.

What is, accordingly, critical is the rate of emotional development within the Church itself. This will determine the position of the new party, whether it is to be a Church party in the old Latin American sense or an independent Christian party implementing modern Catholic social teaching, on the side of the people against privilege.

+ − + −   5

+ − + − *Abortive Social*
Revolution—Bolivia

BOLIVIA WAS THE NEXT LATIN AMERI-
can country to repeat Mexico's experience of a social revolution.
The backgrounds were extremely different, and so have been the
incidents of their respective revolutions. But there is a basic similarity between the first factors of each equation, the breaking down
of the power of a traditional ruling class in order to establish a new
social equilibrium. Bolivia was far more backward and poorer than
Mexico to start, and its revolution began much more recently. It
is consequently impossible to say at this point whether or not a
viable new society will replace the one destroyed.

Bolivia, only a name on the map to many people, is one of the bigger Latin American republics, more than half the size of Mexico, or about as big as Texas and California combined. Most of the slightly more than three million inhabitants live in the Andes mountains, with the biggest concentration on the *altiplano*, a level plateau extending for hundreds of miles at an elevation of more than two miles above sea level.

Bolivia ranks low among Latin American countries in terms of gross national product, literacy, life expectancy, or any of the usual indices. Wealth was concentrated in a small ruling group, with almost everyone else living in misery. Within the general population, however, there was and is a social distinction which must be clarified in order to appreciate what has happened. The distinction is between Indians and mestizos.

Mestizo, or mixed, is a word which might reasonably be taken to mean a person of mixed blood and as such convey a racial connotation. This was how it was originally applied in Latin America, to signify the child born of a white and an Indian. In Bolivia, as generally in Latin America, the intermingling of the races has continued for so many hundred years that while it is easy to distinguish the extreme of Indian and of white, the whole middle mass is so thoroughly mixed as to have assumed the external characteristics of a separate race.

However, the significant point is no longer the race identification. In Bolivia, as in other countries with important unassimilated Indian populations, the essential difference today is cultural. Accordingly, an Indian is one who has not become integrated into Western civilization. He wears native dress, follows tribal habits, and speaks a native dialect. A mestizo is one who has become integrated, even though last year he was an Indian. In passing, it is interesting that in Bolivia the word *blanco* (white) rather than mestizo is used to identify this segment of the population, but mestizo seems less confusing for the American reader. According to this division, more than half of all Bolivians are Indians. More than half of the Indians speak Quechua, and more than a third speak Aymara, but each of these languages has many dialects which are not always mutually intelligible, a language diversity which creates a big communications problem.

The system of Reductions established by the Church with such success in Paraguay and northern Argentina in the early days of the Conquest with the triple function of protecting the Indians from exploitation, improving their living levels, and instructing them in the faith, was introduced also in Bolivia. Soon, however, the colonizers won out over the missionaries, and particularly after the expulsion of the Jesuits in 1767, the hacienda system developed to a degree which made the Indians the serfs of the landowners, obliged to give unpaid labor in return for the right to grow enough food for themselves and their families.

This system continued undisturbed right down to our own days. But back in the early 1930's, Bolivia fought a bloody war for three years with neighboring Paraguay over the ownership of the Chaco province. Both underpopulated countries were bled white, Bolivia losing 60,000 lives and Paraguay 40,000, before Bolivia relinquished her claim. Earlier, however, she had taken a desperate step which has proved to have totally unforeseen results. So acute was the need for recruits that, for the first time in history, the Indians were called on by the upper class and by the mestizos to join them as soldiers and to fight alongside them against the common enemy of the fatherland. For the Indians, the experience proved catalytic. They understandably served as the lowest echelon in the army, but they moved away from their villages, saw how people lived elsewhere, and listened with delighted amazement to the propaganda designed to persuade them that they formed a single nation with other Bolivians, subject to the same obligations and entitled to the same rights. They went back to their homes and their misery with the rest of their defeated brothers-in-arms, but—as events soon proved—things would never be the same again.

The disillusionment that followed the defeat combined with world depression and the general unrest of leftist and rightist ideologies flowing from troubled Europe to develop among the students and other intellectuals of Bolivia a series of movements, some of the extreme left with Socialist and Marxist ideas, others of the far right proclaiming themselves nationalist and anti-imperialist. In what at the time seemed a strange marriage, but not surprising to anyone who understands the ideological closeness of the extreme right and extreme left, these groups combined in 1940 under Victor Paz Estenssoro to initiate a series of violent coups and countercoups. In spite of magnificent programs of reform, the stock in trade of the Latin American revolutionary, there is little doubt that no intention existed of introducing any radical change in the Bolivian social system. If the new group could stabilize itself in power and get a share for itself and its followers in the Government pork barrel, the economic monopoly of the small upper class would continue undisturbed.

At this point, however, the Indians entered the picture. An essential element in the system of Reductions, as introduced in the sixteenth century, was resettlement of the Indians in villages dominated by a Spanish town. When that system broke down, the Indians remained on in the villages, a feature which particularly distinguishes the Cochabamba area. The villages continued to be much more influenced by the neighboring Spanish towns than are the Indians still scattered in the high Andes of Bolivia, Peru and Ecuador. The village Indians had reason to regard themselves as closer to the status of the mestizos, and some of the veterans of the Chaco War had no sooner been demobilized than they determined in effect to change their status to that of mestizo, forming an association to free themselves from the feudal obligations to the landlord. In 1936, the syndicate—as they called their association—leased holdings from some landlords to permit its members to work the land without having to give the traditional unpaid services. They did not object to paying rent. What they wanted was personal freedom, plus the opportunity to keep for themselves any improvements they might introduce. The old system effectively excluded improvement because the landlord got everything over and above the bare requirements for living.

When it looked as if the syndicate might succeed and encourage imitation by other Indians, some of the landlords became worried. In 1939, five of them bought title to the lands which had been rented to the syndicate, cancelled the leases, and cleared large areas by destroying the homes of the Indians, driving away those who had enjoyed immemorial squatter rights unless they agreed to accept a sharecropper agreement similar to the old system. This put an end to the syndicate's attempt to alter the landholding system in a peaceful manner. The organization, however, did not die out. It regrouped in the community of Ucureña, and in the late 1940's it began to re-emerge as a political force under the leadership of a young man named José Rojas, whose father had been driven from his holding by the landlords in 1939. Rojas had in the interval (as mentioned earlier) lived in Argentina and been indoctrinated with Marxist ideas. Identifying himself completely with his fellow Indians, even to the point of affecting to know only Quechua, he rapidly gained undisputed control of his own area, then trained organizers and sent them to form syndicates in Indian villages all over Bolivia. The stage was set for a nation-wide revolt.

Meanwhile the traditional tug of war between the intellectuals and the upper class had continued in the capital. News of Indian unrest was not taken too seriously at first. As a condescending gesture, the government in 1952 announced that it intended to apply the controls on landlords which had been decreed ten years earlier, controls designed to curb their exploitation of their peons.

Everyone knew that the words were a mere formality, but this time everyone included the Indian syndicates, and they were ready for a test of strength. Accordingly, in November 1952, the Ucureña syndicate demanded the return of eleven parcels of land to the Indians who had been driven from an estate a few years earlier. The landlord's refusal brought a call for a general uprising of Indians of several provinces and threats to pillage and burn many towns. Shocked into action, the central government decided its best hope of survival was to get on the band wagon and agree to a broad principle of transfer to Indian ownership of the land in areas of predominantly Indian population. The Indians were not, however, prepared even to wait for an orderly translation of this principle into legislation and administrative action. Instead, the syndicates moved into immediate action and took over the estates within reach, dividing the land among their members and expropriating the estate houses, machinery, vehicles and stock. The big houses became village or syndicate headquarters, schools, hospitals. Any landlords who were around fled to the cities.

It only remained for the government to recognize the fact, and this was done by a decree of August 1953, signed with elaborate ceremony by the president and his entire cabinet before a huge assembly of Indians in the village of Ucureña. All the government could do was try to soften the blow to the national economy. Inefficient as was the old hacienda system, it produced a substantial surplus of food for the cities and of commercial crops for export. Would the Indians, accustomed to a bare subsistence living in which money played almost no part, bother to produce more than they needed for themselves?

The decree tried to hedge against this danger by making provi-

sion in the reform for retention of efficient agricultural units regardless of size. The test was to be efficiency of operation. The
semi-feudal estate lying idle, or exploited inefficiently with obso-
lete tools and with practices tending to perpetuate serfdom, became subject to expropriation in its entirety. But agricultural enterprises, no matter how big, were approved, provided they were operated with large capital investment per unit of land, produced a
cash crop for sale in the market, paid the workers in money and
allowed them to organize and to participate in collective bargaining.

Indian communities were authorized by the decree to recover
lands wrongly taken from them, and those claiming restitution
rights might occupy immediately the land to which they had
claims. The provision, a strange one, reveals the true nature of the
situation. Those who had already moved in could not be dispossessed, nor could others be held back while the landlord fought a
delaying action in the law courts.

No serious effort was made to establish a cooperative or collective ownership like that introduced in Mexico under its land reform. What the Bolivian Indian wanted was his own plot of land,
and the decree met this situation by conferring on every citizen
over eighteen years of age the right to a grant wherever land was
available, provided he cultivated his claim within two years, with
preference given to those who were already farmers and already
resident in the area where the land was located.

The same political realism which had made the government recognize and legalize the fact of seizure of the land by the Indians
compelled it to carry out another electoral promise and nationalize
the tin mines, the second base of the wealth and power of the
upper class. Through these two actions, the small upper class has
practically disappeared, many of its members leaving the country
entirely either voluntarily or under pressure.

Even if such extreme changes had not occurred, the Bolivian economy would have had tough sledding during the past ten years. Minerals account for nearly all of the country's exports, with tin providing by far the biggest part. The Korean War shot up the price of tin, resulting in a great increase in the number of tin workers added to the payroll for political reasons. In 1951, the United States cut its tin purchases substantially, an action which began a violent fall in the price of the metal. Meanwhile, costs of production were rising because of exhaustion of some of the high-bearing deposits. The combination of all these factors provoked an unparalleled inflation which in five years brought the boliviano from 60 to about 12,000 to the dollar, and this in turn wiped out much accumulated wealth and put another nail in the coffin of the old upper class. Only a constant flow of United States aid, at a level higher than that for any other Latin American country (a total of $170 million between 1952 and 1962), has kept the economy functioning in an orderly way and prevented a total economic collapse. Much of the aid has been given in pursuance of planned programs intended to put Bolivia on a sound basis by developing the country's productive capacity, but such long-term aims are not being realized. In fact, the money is used to keep the country alive, and there is every reason to assume that massive direct subsidization of Bolivia will be needed for many years to come.

What conclusions should be drawn from the events of the past ten years in Bolivia? I think the most important is the evidence it provides of the impossibility of continuing the hacienda system anywhere in Latin America. The Indians have reached a point where they are not going to endure much longer the obvious injustices of their subhuman lot. All it will take to provoke like reactions in other countries is some small incident of the kind that produced the explosion in Bolivia. Nor do I think we can always count on a take-over by the Indians with so little bloodshed as in

Bolivia. On the contrary, it is easy to conceive a situation such as might have occurred in Bolivia if the government had decided to fight rather than try to ride with the Indian revolt, a bloody and endless civil war ranging the mestizos against the Indians.

What is also significant is the rapid development of internal Indian leadership. Ever since the Conquest, the Indian has been protected and controlled, and even the pre-Conquest civilizations gave the masses little personal freedom and discretion. Nevertheless, the Indians of Bolivia quickly rallied round one of their own, José Rojas, and he in turn was able to train assistants and form a wide net of syndicates capable of taking concerted action.

Most interesting of all is the definition of aims and goals by the newly created self-determining communities into which the former landlord-controlled hacienda villages have transformed themselves. First of all, they have become what is in effect a new class, intermediate between their former status as Indians and the mestizos, with below them a class still recognized as Indians in remote places that have not been absorbed into the new patterns. To mark this change, they have adopted a new name for themselves. They are no longer called Indians but *campesinos* or peasants.

Previously, an Indian could move upwards as an individual into the mestizo class by leaving his highland community to live in a mestizo community and adopt as many as possible of the mestizo class symbols, the Spanish language, Western dress, and so on. Now, however, for the first time since the Reductions, an Indian community is moving as a group upward into the Western way of life, so that it will gradually take on most of the culture characteristics of the mestizos without having to break violently with its own past. Accordingly, while the peasants live in the same houses as before and eat the same food, they have acquired a new attitude toward education. Many villages have built a school, the condition for getting a government teacher. Their children dress in the

school uniforms which were formerly worn only by the children of
Spanish-speaking mestizos, and this change in turn encourages the
other members of the family to move toward the Western fashion
in clothing.

As I have tried to stress, it is still too soon to draw definite conclusions about the real effects of the transformation of peasant life
in Bolivia. However, I have found a widespread optimism among
many observers. It was confidently asserted, they point out, that
the Indians would start off their independent existence by slaughtering and eating the cattle on the haciendas, by allowing the land
to erode and exhaust itself, by failing to keep enough corn or po-
tatoes for seed for next year's planting. None of these things happened. Instead, there was a quick increase in the amount of food
they kept for themselves and in the amount they sent to market.
Perhaps part of the increase was merely apparent, for there was
no longer the need to hide from the landlord whatever portion of
the crop it was possible to conceal, and to sell it in a black market.
But each year has shown steady increases in production which are
considerably higher than the rate of population increase and accordingly represent a rising standard of living.

A complicating factor, though a basically encouraging one, is
that the felt needs of the newly emancipated Indians have been
expanding at a more rapid rate than their productive capacity.
Everyone, for example, wants a bicycle, and today there are tens
of thousands of bicycles in Indian villages which formerly did not
have even one. Similarly, sewing machines are becoming common-
place. Desirable as is such a development in itself, there are obvious economic dangers, which are also capable in Bolivia's conditions today of expressing themselves in political violence, in the
existence of demands substantially greater than the economy's ability to satisfy, all the more so when facilities for borrowing at reasonable interest rates are scant. National consumption far in excess

of national production is a basic cause of the desperate inflation and of the depreciation in the external value of the currency, and it is also a major reason for the failure to gain the long-term benefits which United States aid was intended to assure. Nevertheless, the threat of political upheaval because of the conscious sense of deprivation, a sense which extremist political leaders have consistently exploited, compels the United States to continue its aid, even if results are no more than stopgap.

It cannot be assumed that the Bolivian revolution has run its course and will now settle into an era of reconstruction similar to the one in Mexico. Ill-prepared as were the Mexicans for the great leap forward from the sixteenth to the twentieth century, they were vastly more ready than are the Bolivians. Even if the proclaimed objective of the revolution in Mexico was to project the Indian into civilized life, he never became a prime mover in the process. At all times, the initiative remained in the hands of people with some background of education and sophistication, and with enough stake in the existing order to urge moderation in transforming it. Mexico had also reached a vastly more advanced point of economic development, with high living standards and a higher level of literacy and adaptation to modern ways when its revolution occurred. The emotional climate throughout the world today is much more violent than then. There is little basic community of interest between the Bolivian mestizos who control the machinery of government and the peasant Indians who have proved their ability to overthrow a ruling class and who any day may decide that their new masters are a small improvement on the old.

+ − + −   6

+ − + − *Perverted Social*
Revolution—Cuba

Mexico's revolution has shown
that social change is possible, even if it involves elimination of foreign control of critical areas of the economy, without lasting harm
to United States interests, whether political or commercial. Bolivia
is demonstrating the dangers of letting a situation deteriorate to
the point of explosion. And the most recent social revolution in
Latin America carries yet another lesson. In Cuba we see how dam-
aging for our commercial interests and our world position such a
movement becomes when it is driven, whether by individuals or
events, into an open challenge of the United States.

What went wrong in Cuba? Perhaps it is more pertinent to ask
what was wrong in Cuba. Many things were wrong. From the time

the island won its independence at the turn of the century, it never enjoyed any long period of good government. Indeed, Cubans had reconciled themselves to venal and self-seeking politicians, and were grateful if robbery of public funds was not too blatant.

Unlike Mexico and Bolivia, Cuba had no class of unassimilated Indians, but like them and like most Latin America, it had a small upper class enjoying great wealth and privilege, while the masses lived in ignorance and misery. An unusual feature of its agriculture was that American companies owned many of the sugar fields and factories from which the island derived most of its foreign exchange.

Fulgencio Batista operated for many years very much like other dictators who had ruled Cuba. He was a little more lenient than some, for at the instance of the Bishop of Santiago, he spared the life of a young firebrand who had led an assault on a military fort. It proved for him a grave error. Fidel Castro was no sooner out of jail than he began to plot again. Before long, he was head of a small band of guerillas in the Oriente mountains. By all accounts, the group was of no military significance. But its public relations was effective. The idea of David challenging Goliath captured the public imagination both within and outside Cuba. Batista was in trouble.

His answer was to tighten the screws on the people. For two years, Cuba endured a reign of terror which welded the whole of the people as never before into a national unity. Their union rested on a very limited base—to get rid of the tyranny. But it was enough to secure its objective. The collapse of Batista came not from the strength of Castro but from his own weakness. Abandoned by everyone, he was lucky to escape alive.

Castro's first acts on coming to power confirmed in the minds of Cubans the good opinions he had gained as Batista's enemy.

In particular, they were delighted at the formation of a government of obviously honest men. This is one aspect of the Castro
regime which nobody seems ever to have called into question.
Whether Castro himself was dishonest by deceiving the people as
to his real intentions is still a moot question, but the absence of
graft and self-enrichment is a characteristic which for the first time
has been revealed in a Cuban government.

A disturbing element entered with the setting up of revolutionary courts totally alien to the Latin American tradition and un-
pleasantly savoring of the excesses of the reign of terror of the
French Revolution and the people's courts of Soviet Russia and
China. Yet there was no doubt about the guilt of great numbers
of Batista's henchmen, and it was plausible to argue that the only
way to prevent the outraged Cubans from taking the law into their
own hands and slaughtering thousands was to prove to them that
the new regime would punish the guilty, and to make the point
by quick justice to some hundreds of the ringleaders.

The next big milestone in the evolution of the regime was the
publication in May 1959, five months after it came to power, of
a law for agrarian reform. This quickly gave rise to most heated
discussion both in Cuba and in the United States, in both of
which it was rightly regarded as heralding a definite break with the
past and the inauguration—if it were implemented—of a change
as basic as that which had occurred in Mexico and Bolivia.

Nevertheless, this law did not answer the question of whether or
not Castro was engaged on a program of bringing Cuba into the
Communist camp. It is easy to be wise with hindsight. But those
who were close to the events could only call them as they saw
them. When I was in Cuba in June 1958, six months before the
Batista collapse, I made contact with leading elements of Catholic
Action, which had been a powerful movement some years earlier
but had been forced by Batista's fear of all organizations to sus-

pend open activity and lead a furtive existence. These people were convinced that a normal life for the country and the Church could come about only with the overthrow of Batista. They were convinced, moreover, that a Castro victory would bring with it this normal life, though they regarded a clear-cut military victory as unlikely and anticipated a government formed by a coalition of professional politicians which would offer a program acceptable to Castro's idealists. They denied vehemently my suggestion that statements made by Castro reflected left-wing or anticlerical attitudes, assuring me that on the contrary many of his advisers and lieutenants were militant Catholics, former Catholic Actionists, and that a government headed by him would be friendly to the Church.

I was again in Cuba a year later in June 1959, the month after the publication of the text of the agrarian reform law. Already, people were beginning to get worried. An important segment of conservative Catholicism had broken with Castro, charging that the provisions of this law were contrary to Catholic teaching and would lead the country to Communism. The more socially-minded Catholics did not agree, and they had vocal support from the hierarchy. Archbishop Evilio Diaz, for example, declared in a pastoral issued shortly after the publication of the text of the law that every Catholic "as a good Cuban and a better Christian" was bound to help implement its provisions.

In Cuba, as elsewhere in Latin America, almost all the good land was owned by a few landlords who lived in the capital and brought to the capital the wealth they extracted from their estates. Accordingly, in this nation slightly smaller than the State of Pennsylvania, with ten million acres of pastures and five million of rich cultivated land and abundant mineral wealth, the vast majority of the six million inhabitants lived in abject poverty. Poverty pressed particularly hard on the rural workers. Half a million of them depended on sugar for a livelihood, but only about one in ten had year-round employment at an annual average wage in recent years of about $450. The others worked according to the seasonal demands of sugar, from 65 to 105 days a year, earning a total of $100 to $200.

The masses were not only poor but also largely illiterate and without anyone to express their views and needs, until Castro came along. And they were growing in numbers at a more rapid rate than that of the absorptive capacity of the economy. Each year the work in the sugar fields and mills had to be spread over more men, and that meant less money for each. The sugar industry was capable of rapid expansion to probably ten million tons annually, but the level was artificially controlled at about six to seven million, because this was all that could be sold under international agreements. No doubt the decision was a proper economic one to make, but it certainly did nothing to endear the under-employed worker to the big corporations which owned or controlled most of the sugar land with some three-fifths of the capital in United States hands and nearly another fifth in other foreign ownership.

Cubans of all classes had always agreed that social reform would have to begin with land redistribution to ensure wider ownership and end absentee landlordism. Cuba's national hero, José Martí, proclaimed as the fourth of his "ten commandments" of the revolution in 1895 the need for agrarian reform. "The land that has many smallholders is rich," he wrote. No politician ever challenged that statement. To question Martí in Cuba would be more suicidal for a politician than to question Jefferson in the United States.

But neither did anyone try to implement the principle, not until Castro in 1959. Three years earlier, Dr. Julio Morales, national president of Catholic Action, presented a code of land reform in Congress. It was a modest project, but it would have begun division of the estates among the landless, and given them credit and technical help to set them up as small farmers. The landlords, men who would be insulted if anyone questioned their Catholicity, joined with the corrupt politicians to quash the project.

The Castro plan was much more sweeping. It provided for splitting up the estates into holdings of (usually) 64 acres, leaving a unit of approximately one thousand acres to the former owner. Value was to be established on the basis of current tax valuations, the owner to be paid in 4½ per cent bonds with the income from the bonds tax-exempt for ten years if invested in new Cuban industries. In addition, corporations might grow sugar only if all stockholders were Cubans, and no stockholder in such corporations might hold stock in or operate Cuban sugar mills.

None of the provisions was particularly novel, and all fitted into the "eminent domain" concept under which all governments, including our own, expropriate property for reasons of common benefit. Indeed all of them, except the special provisions for sugar operations, were practically identical with the procedures under which the near-totality of the agricultural land of Ireland, north and south, has been transferred during the past century from absentee landlords to tenant occupiers. Not only was there nothing unorthodox in the proposal to pay for expropriated lands in bonds rather than cash, but there is no alternative way. No government has resources, other than the printing press, to make payments of the magnitude involved, and the impact on the economy would be equally harmful if such quantities of cash were suddenly released internally, or if they were exported by the landlords (as they might well be), leaving the country decapitalized. Japan's land reform under United States military government after World War II made payment in bonds.

Also similar to the Irish Land Commission was the National Institute of Agrarian Reform (INRA), charged with the mechanics of the land transfer. In Ireland, the Land Commission was given

substantial control over the use, division or sale of property during
the long period allowed the new owner to pay off the purchase
price in annual installments. The theory was that a man with no
experience as an independent operator might ruin the land by
neglect, mortgage it to money lenders, or initiate excessive fragmentation by subdividing among his sons.

The same reasoning applied with more force in Cuba. Illiterate
peasants unskilled in the techniques of modern farming might
cause a serious drop in the already inadequate crop production,
run into debt and lose their holdings. To guard against such possibilities, the law provided that INRA would give only a qualified
title to the new owners, preventing the sale or pledging as col-
lateral of the land, and even restricting the transfer by inheritance.
The Institute was charged with organizing cooperatives to provide
farm machinery on a contract basis, an absolutely necessary element in the modernization of small holdings. In addition, it was
authorized to exercise many controls, including the power to direct
specific uses of the land in various situations.

That danger exists with such controls is undeniable, but I do
not think that they were *a priori* unreasonable in the circumstances, and they certainly represented a far less onerous burden
on the intended beneficiaries than the controls traditionally exercised by the Latin American landlord over his peons, or than did
the encomienda system established earlier by the Spanish state and
Church to civilize the Indians. I think it essential to keep these
things in perspective. The limited proprietorship promised to the
Cuban peasant by Castro's law represented for him an immense
step forward. That was how he understood it, and that was how a
major part of Cuban opinion—including Cuba's Catholic opinion
—understood. There is not a landless peasant in the length and
breadth of Latin America who would not think himself unspeaka-
bly blessed to be made such an offer.

Did Castro ever really intend to carry out this sort of land reform, or to implement any of the other liberal changes which he
had presented to the Cubans as the purpose of his movement? The
question is still hotly debated among those who were close to the
events. Some blame the rapid change in the attitude of the United
States for Castro's about-face. This country had wholeheartedly
sympathized with the bearded revolutionaries in their unequal
struggle with Batista's might. Public outrage had forced our government to adopt an increasingly hostile attitude to Batista,
thereby contributing to his collapse. In conformity with our proclaimed dedication to democracy, we welcomed the promise of
elections and the abolition of censorship. But when it became apparent that Castro intended to go much further than restore the
forms of democracy, that he proposed an institutional reform of a
kind that we on the level of theory agreed with as an essential
prerequisite to the true functioning of democracy, we drew back.
The next step threatened United States economic interests, and
soon the loudest voices in this country were those who were shout-
ing that payment in cash must precede expropriation of United
States-owned land in Cuba.

I do not know if a different attitude on our part would have
affected Castro's program. There are strong indications now that
he planned all along what he actually did, deceiving not only us
but his own people with cunning shamelessness. I do, however,
believe that the United States government and the United States
press served this country and the cause of freedom very badly by
failing to isolate and define the issues, and by presenting the
United States position as a defence of the wealthy against the poor,
of the strong against the weak. If our government then had the
intelligence to offer a full partnership in a program to bring into
existence in Cuba the kind of society we have been telling the
Latins for years they need, it would at least have taken the wind

out of Castro's sails, if we assume that it was always his intention to establish a Communist dictatorship. Not only would the task have been vastly more difficult for him in Cuba but in the rest of Latin America he would have been exposed in his true colors, instead of being made a martyr to the most popular of Latin American causes: self-defence against the aggressions of the Colossus of the North.

The press failed hopelessly to clarify the issues. With a handful of exceptions, editors in leading articles repeated the fatuous nonsense churned out to them in statements of the National Association of Manufacturers and the National Foreign Trade Council about the sacred rights of the noble-minded investor who risks his life savings overseas for the benefit of the underprivileged of other lands. Columnists recalled nostalgically the good old days when civilization was safe on Carib isles under the bayonets of the Marines. Reporters selected news to suit the positions already adopted by their publishers, presenting as fact the biased third-hand claims of interested parties, or accepted the humiliation of having their objectionable facts censored out on the copy desk.

Whoever or whatever was to blame for the gulf that quickly opened between the Castro revolution and the United States, whether it was caused by our failure to understand, to sympathize, to support, or by Castro's determination to break with the West and establish a Socialist type dictatorship, expropriating $1.5 billion worth of United States property in the process, it was inevitable that once he began to move away from us he would be drawn by the force of events into the Soviet camp. Russia and her allies are taking Cuba's exports and providing the capital and consumer goods needed to maintain the economy. Their technicians have replaced those of the United States in industry, commerce and education. They are helping the internal Communists to build a Soviet system. The press is completely captive. Private education has been destroyed, and state schools begin with Communist indoctrination. Young Cubans who go abroad to study are sent to schools and universities behind the Iron Curtain. In the country, the so-called cooperatives have become the machinery to collectivize farming, and the Institute of Agrarian Reform has grown into a gigantic organization holding title to more than half the land of Cuba and dominating the lives of the peasants. Industry has been taken over at an equally rapid pace. The old army has been replaced by a revolutionary militia far larger in numbers and far more indoctrinated in ideology and loyalty.

Some background is necessary to understand the role of the Catholic Church during these events, and their effect on it. Although the first diocese was created in 1518 and the island was a Spanish possession—except for a year or two—until 1898, the Church did not flourish as in other Spanish possessions. Cuba was considered primarily a transit point. During the seventeenth and eighteenth centuries, religious life was disturbed by clashes with the civil authority, a shortage of priests and prolonged absences of bishops. One does not find in Cuba the magnificent colonial churches which adorn Mexico, Colombia, Peru and other countries. Although a university under Church auspices and a seminary were established in the eighteenth century, the effect on Catholic life was not profound. On the contrary, these intellectual centers developed a narrow aristocratic culture, tending to independence of the Holy See, with rationalist and Jansenist elements derived from the Encyclopedists and the freethinkers of the French Revolution. Later, most of the clergy backed the Spanish regime against the Cubans who sought to free their country. Many parishes were abandoned and many churches destroyed, and national independence arrived in a climate of religious indifference.

Particularly after World War II, a new sense of the role of the Church in both the spiritual and social fields developed among lay intellectuals organized in Catholic Action. Among their activities was a survey of religious conditions and attitudes in Cuba carried out in a very scientific way by the university section of Catholic Action. The four thousand persons interviewed did not even know that the interviewers were Catholics. Some suspected that certain questions they were asked were Communist-inspired. One scandalized lady chased the interviewer from her home when he asked her if she believed that Jesus Christ was divine.

This survey helps to explain some of the things that North Americans find most perplexing about Catholicism in Latin America, and it also helps to explain why an overwhelmingly Catholic country like Cuba or Mexico can endure a government openly hostile to the faith.

While 90 per cent of Cubans were baptized Catholics, when the study was made, about one in five was openly indifferent, although for traditional reasons he sought or permitted his children to be baptized. One of every three adult Catholics never made his First Communion, and only one in four fulfilled the Easter precept. Very many marriages lacked canonical validity, and considerably more than half of all Cuban Catholics approved of divorce.

Religious ignorance was appalling. Only two Cubans out of three believed that Christ was God, or that the human soul was immortal, or that hell existed. Fewer believed in purgatory. Confining the investigation to a few basic doctrines of the Catholic faith, at most two out of three Catholics in Cuba could be considered orthodox, while expanding the investigation to include (for example) divorce, dropped the number to perhaps less than one in three. Most, however, did not realize that their beliefs were at variance with their obligations as Catholics.

Superstitions were revealed to be flourishing. One Cuban in a hundred gave spirit worship or a similar African cult as his sole religion, the proportion rising sharply in remote areas where there were few priests. The Bayamo district, for example, had two priests and ten spirit-worship centers. Here one inhabitant in nine gave spirit worship as his sole religion. Vast numbers of others mixed primitive jungle rites with the Christianity they professed, to the point that one Cuban in four admitted having gone at some time to placate the spirits or get their advice.

Although Cuba had been more exposed than most parts of Latin America to Protestant missionaries, they had won relatively few adherents, about 5 per cent of the population, in spite of the fact that Protestant ministers outnumbered Catholic priests by three to two, even before the Castro persecution cut the number of priests substantially, and three out of every four Protestant ministers were Cubans. Professing Protestants are found principally in the very lowest social and economic groups, that is to say, among the most ignorant. The major effect of their missionary efforts among other groups has been to increase indifferentism. The province most proselytized by Protestantism was Matanzas, where it had many schools. Urban Protestants here constituted 6.5 per cent, not much higher than the island average, but the rural proportion rose to 14 per cent. What was most striking, however, was the number of religiously indifferent persons in Matanzas, nearly one in four, indicating that the main effect of the proselytizing activity was to disturb the religious beliefs of the Catholics.

Freemasonry was also quite strong in Cuba, and it had succeeded in creating for itself a favorable image in the minds of Cubans, including Catholic Cubans. Of people who told the Catholic Action interviewers that they were Catholics, 3 per cent immediately went on to admit that they were Freemasons. Another 45 per cent said they were not Freemasons but would have no objection to joining, while only 3 per cent of the Catholics asserted definitely that they would not join. Very many Cuban Freemasons think of the lodge as a social or mutual aid institution, rather like Rotary or the Lions. There has always, however, been a hard core of anticlerical and anti-religious Masons, and most of the recurrent attacks on Catholic principles came from the ranks of organized Freemasonry. As recently as 1956, a virulent campaign was waged against the Church's stand on Christian moral teaching in the schools.

Social position and education were also reflected in the religious statistics. The survey revealed that 67 per cent of the lowest class were Catholics, 82 per cent of the lower middle class, 88 per cent of the upper middle class, and almost 100 per cent of the upper class. Similarly, only 42 per cent of illiterates rated inclusion as Catholics, a percentage which rose to 91 for those with secondary schooling, then fell off to 70 for college level (mainly because of the naturalistic and materialistic teaching at the University of Havana).

As is general throughout Latin America, priests were few in relation to the population: six million people and 700 priests, of whom some three-quarters were foreign born, most of them from Spain. A great improvement in this respect had begun at about the same time as Catholic Action was introduced. In twenty years the number of vocation centers doubled from five to ten, three of them being for the diocesan clergy, the other seven for religious orders and congregations of men. Between them, they numbered nearly 500 seminarists when Castro came to power.

Catholics joined with other Cubans in welcoming the triumph of the Castro revolution. It was not simply that they rejoiced at the end of the sufferings they had endured under the dictator. Many of them looked forward to the implementation of the social program proclaimed from the Sierra Maestra, for educated young Catholics had become profoundly imbued with the social message of recent Popes. Soon, however, the older Catholics, especially those belonging to the upper class, became frightened, and raised loud protesting voices. The bishops, nevertheless, leant over backwards in their anxiety to find common ground. They expressed their delight at the early steps to restore a system of political liberty and social progress, at the abolition of censorship, the revival of Catholic organizations, the cleaning up of the traditionally corrupt government machinery.

Even when hidden Communist influences began to show through the action of the government, and to express themselves in totalitarian policies, they made every effort to mobilize opinion against the defects without challenging the government's good faith and intentions. A series of episcopal statements analyzed Communism and warned of its dangers without ever pointing the finger directly at the Castro regime. But even indirect criticism was more than Castro would tolerate. A collective pastoral of August 1960 praising what the government had done to help the poor but pointing out the harm that could flow from increasing Communist influence was the signal for an anti-religious campaign of national dimensions. Several priests were arrested for reading this pastoral from their pulpits, and others were threatened with "popular reprisals" if they read it. In the villages meetings were organized in which the priest was insulted and derided. Catholic programs on radio and television were suppressed. Pseudo-Catholic fronts were created.

All of these and many further examples were listed in a pastoral signed by all Cuba's bishops and dated December 4, 1960, in which for the first time they charged the regime directly with attempting to stifle the Church, declaring also that Castro personally could not escape responsibility for these attacks, because of his calumnious statements about the work of the Church in Cuba.

Castro reacted in typical fashion, devoting the major part of a nearly four-hour televised speech to a vituperative denunciation of the bishops as hypocrites and liars. "What has my agrarian reform got to do with the Blessed Sacrament? Let them amuse themselves with their silly practices and leave me to help the people. . . ."

His explosion triggered a chain reaction. The magazine *Bohemia* (like all surviving publications, operated by the regime) called Cardinal Spellman a protector of criminals and thieves, adding in an apoplectically mixed metaphor that Yankee imperialism and the imperialism of the Holy See "are nothing more, especially in Latin America, than two faces of the same phenomenon long condemned as inhuman and fallacious." The newspaper *El Mundo* published a letter from the Federation of University Students (another regime mouthpiece), charging the priests with betraying Christ.

From this point there was no return. During 1961, the regime completed the take-over of all educational institutions, including the Catholic University of Villanueva, and of the remaining Catholic publications. Large numbers of priests were driven from the country, many of them under the pretext that they were foreigners, but even those who were natural-born Cuban nationals were not spared.

Following the techniques used by the Communists in East Europe and in China, pseudo-religious organizations were created and headed by dissident Catholics, including a priest long under permanent suspension, Germán Lence. Typical of regime support of this renegade was publication prominently in various newspapers of a photostatic copy of a letter signed by a Monsignor José E. Xavier Cortés, Vicar General, and bearing the seal of the Metropolitan Archbishopric of Mexico. The letter caused great confusion to many Cuban Catholics, as it was intended that it should, for it declared that the bishops of Mexico congratulated Father Germán Lence for having publicly urged Cuban Catholics to prevent the reading of a pastoral letter from their own bishops in the churches. The controlled radio and television gave broad further publication to this document. What was concealed, and what the regime's monopoly of communications kept from the public, was that "Monsignor" Cortés is not only not vicar general of a Catholic archdiocese in Mexico but not even a Catholic priest. He is a Mexican who many years ago falsified ordination documents, substituting his name for that of another, and who worked in Cuba for two years before being unmasked, and is again operating out of Mexico.

The open declaration in December 1961 of Castro's adherence to Marxism-Leninism means that the Catholic Church can anticipate continuing persecution for as long as his regime remains in power. It also, of course, meant a clarification of the position of Castro's Cuba in the East-West struggle. The clarification was not, however, as complete or decisive in its effect on other Latin American governments as the United States expected it would be. The special meeting of American foreign ministers at Punta del Este, Uruguay, in February 1962, summoned by the United States in the confident belief that it could persuade the Latin Americans to join it in a clear-cut condemnation and humiliation of Castro for having openly proclaimed himself a Communist, demonstrated rather how much magic he still possesses. The best the State Department could achieve was support by a technical two-thirds majority, the minimum necessary for passage, of a greatly watered down resolution. The six countries which opposed exclusion of Castro's regime from the Organization of American States and abstained from voting included the three major Latin American powers, Argentina, Brazil and Mexico. Between them, the six abstaining countries contain more than two-thirds of all Latin Americans.

As I see it, the way the United States won its victory is even more serious than its technical nature. Great moral damage was caused to us among Latin Americans by the public announcement by members of our delegation on arrival at the conference that the future of the Alliance for Progress program hung on its outcome. During the conference it was publicly asserted, though obviously not on the record, that Haiti was holding out for a bigger share of Alliance funds as the price of its vote, a vote without which even the technical two-thirds majority was impossible. President Kennedy, when announcing the Alliance for Progress, had insisted that this program had to depend exclusively on the willingness of Latin American nations to introduce needed economic and social reforms. To create the impression, as the United States delegates did, that what matters is support of our political positions, not only vitiates the program itself but convinces Latin Americans that nothing has changed, that principles are meaningless to the United States, that we can always be counted on to make a deal if the price is right.

One thing that must be obvious is that Castro remains a force throughout Latin America, and this not only among the extreme left-wingers who are happy to accept his Communism. Those who have nothing to lose, those who have given up hope of peaceful social reform, those who believe the United States still regards Latin America as its sphere of political and economic influence, to be exploited for its benefit, those who seek a means to blackmail the United States into giving bigger handouts, those who admire the courage of the small boy sticking out his tongue at the teacher, all of these and many others combine to maintain the ambivalence of Latin American attitudes to Castro.

7

+ − + − *Foreign Capital Primes the Pump*

RECENTLY I LUNCHED WITH A MAN who, following a distinguished career in the National Recovery Agency during the Depression, spent many years as a business consultant in Latin America. He startled me by asserting that all of the region's problems could be summed up in two: the international oil companies and the Catholic Church. He did not want to eliminate either of these institutions, for both of which he regarded the need as equally obvious, but he contended that the attitudes and actions of each had much to do with Latin America's stagnation, and that if one could change them, everything else would follow.

I do not at all agree in the sense of blaming either institution for the situation in which Latin America finds itself. Actually, I cannot see that any single group should be chosen as scapegoat. If we take the entire range of human history and the entire extent of the surface of the globe, we find that only an infinitesimal proportion of all the societies and civilizations that have flourished through the years succeeded in providing a substantial level of material and spiritual satisfaction to more than a tiny minority of their peoples. The story of the Spanish and Portuguese colonies in the New World is closer to the average than that of the colonies which grew into the United States. To rejoice at the more rapid flowering of the latter should not be to sneer at the former.

My friend's remark does, nevertheless, seem to me to have a deep significance, especially if we take the oil companies to typify the foreign risk capital which has played a big part in the life of Latin America in this century. Both this capital and the Catholic Church, precisely because they are not and never have been an integral part of this stagnant society, but rather distinct elements interacting with it according to their own laws, are capable of a dynamic role in changing it which it could not itself perform without denying its nature. If neither has performed such a role, it is pertinent to ask why. Let me start with foreign capital, leaving the Church for later consideration.

Mexico taught the oil interests a tactical lesson. Up to the 1930's, foreign capital believed it could dictate the terms on which it operated in Latin America. The oil companies and the other big investing interests determined their methods and goals in whatever way seemed to them to ensure the highest yields, disregarding the effect of their activities on the local economy. They fixed their royalty rates arbitrarily, determined extraction levels and development programs without concern for depletion of non-renewable resources, ignored the effect of wage scales on local living, imported high-cost workers and excluded local labor from good jobs, paid imported employees higher scales than local men who performed the same function.

When Mexico challenged this technique of exploitation by nationalizing the mines and petroleum deposits, the former owners organized an international boycott with the object of teaching the ingrates a lesson. Unrelated international developments, however, thwarted their purpose. The rise of the hostile power of Nazi Germany and Japan forced the United States to reverse the unfriendly policy it had adopted toward Mexico at the behest of the oil interests. As World War II cut off foreign markets and sources of supply, the United States business community found it necessary to follow its government's lead, to overlook the past and develop new opportunities within the framework of the legislation drafted by Mexico to prevent a repetition of the economic throttlehold previously enjoyed by the oil interests.

Meanwhile, the United States oil interests had found a new area to develop in Latin America, namely, Venezuela. Smarting from their wounds, they approached the new location with a determination to avoid a repetition of their bitter experience. And so they offered a new approach, which has come to be known through an understandable simplification of a complex and flexible arrangement as the 50–50 formula. The basic idea was that the local government would, through a combination of royalties and taxes, retain half the profits resulting from the exploitation of the oil. Various additional expedients sought to establish a favorable image of the foreign company. It undertook major training programs of nationals and progressively opened executive and administrative posts to them. It developed housing, commissariat, health and pension benefits. As a rule, the limiting factor on its benefactions to its employees was the resistance of local business and industry, which protested that the high rates of remuneration were creating dissatisfaction among their own workers, upsetting wage standards and creating a climate of unrest.

British and other international oil interests were at first outraged by Venezuela's 50–50 formula as disruptive of the arrangements they had established in their various backyards. They were nevertheless forced gradually to improve their terms in the Middle East and elsewhere, but they moved too slowly and too little to match the temper and political realities of the world that emerged from World War II. Iran nationalized its oil industry, as Mexico had done. A British boycott and other manipulations forced a change of regime and a compromise solution. But the compromise altered the scales in Iran to a point not only equaling but passing the Venezuelan formula, and further benefits were won by some Middle East oil producers in the following years.

It was once more the turn of the Venezuelans to feel a grievance. Accordingly, they began in the middle 1950's to press their claims for a reopening of the agreements with the idea of establishing a distribution of profits more favorable to them than the 50–50 formula. Business and political sophistication had increased greatly in the underdeveloped world in a quarter of a century. Many countries were asking why they could not control their oil industries and integrate them into their domestic economies, hiring management and skilled operators wherever they might be found.

Unfortunately, the emotional development of the big oil companies had not paralleled that of the countries in which they operated. When faced with the new demands, they had outgrown and forgotten the lessons of Mexico. Besides, they believed (and for the short term, their belief has been justified by the events) that Venezuela could not emancipate itself in the way Mexico had done. Thanks to stepped-up production in the Middle East, a vast new flood of oil from the Sahara, and a steady increase in exports from the Soviet Union, the world was experiencing and would continue for a considerable time to experience a glut of oil. If Venezuela were so foolish as to nationalize the oil industry, it would not get a market at any price. Proof of this self-evident proposition, should it be needed, is at hand in the experience of the company formed by the Venezuelan government to take over concessions surrendered by the oil companies on the expiry of their leases. Although this company has drilled highly successful wells in those areas, it has not succeeded in finding any buyers for the oil.

What I have described is only a part of the oil story, or of the over-all story of foreign capital in Latin America. I have, however, started with it, because I believe it is what the Latin American critic of the role of foreign capital considers as the significant part of the story, and whether he is right or wrong, it is important to understand his viewpoint before we can move forward constructively. This critic brushes aside the huge constructive effort involved in developing Venezuela's oil industry, which is capable of producing four million barrels a day—more than any country in the world other than the United States. He brushes aside the fact that the international companies adjusted their arrangements to give the Venezuelan government 65 per cent of profits, which brings Venezuela into line with what the Middle East secured. He brushes aside what all the international companies have done to modernize and develop the hemisphere, because he believes that they have done what they have done for the sole purpose of getting what they can while giving only what they must.

When the position is presented in those terms, I think that most Americans will agree that such is in fact the principle on which the United States businessman operates, that the application of this very principle is what in fact made the United States great, and that there is no other principle that makes sense in business. Up to a point, he is correct, for the profit motive is the essence of capitalism. We are, nevertheless, faced here with a real dilemma, and our approach to it reflects one of the big differences between North Americans and Latin Americans. For us, the theoretical basis for our position is relatively unimportant. We know that this approach has in fact worked for us, and we are impatient with anyone who tries to make subtle distinctions, even more with anyone who insists on resurrecting and torturing a long and complicated past history.

Nevertheless, in this instance, the present makes no sense, and the future can provide no solution unless we make distinctions and analyze to some extent the historical development. Capitalism has worked for us in the United States and enabled us to create a society of plenty for the great mass of the population only because we modified it by the creation of a whole series of checks and balances to temper the profit motive. We have our elaborate system of curbs on the creation of monopolies and on monopolistic practices; controls over private companies engaged in essential services such as transport and communications; public subsidization of segments of the economy which are sensitive to uncontrolled competition, such as farming; techniques to prevent unfair foreign competition against our industry and business; vast public investment in segments of our economy which private capital is either reluctant to enter or unwilling to operate on conditions which Congress judges necessary in the general interest. We have our powerful trades union organization, now developed to a point where the worker can meet on terms of equality with his employer and present his viewpoints man to man.

I know that many Americans dislike these and other curbs we have introduced, and that they feel that we have gone far beyond the desirable point in restricting the operation of the profit motive. However, that is here beside the point. What concerns them is a matter of degree. Few believe for a moment that the United States economy or society could operate without the FCC or Social Security or organizations to permit collective bargaining. And besides, what we are facing here is the fact that what the Latin American sees is that we have one way of practicing capitalism within the United States and another in Latin America. One way produces a broad-based society of well-being, where any man who wants to work has the opportunity to work, and where every man who works earns enough to maintain himself and his family in decent conditions. The other produces profits for the investor of capital, at least on average, and it benefits a segment of the economy of the country in which it operates. But its benefits are restricted narrowly. In Venezuela, for example, the oil worker is very well off, but the excessive development of the oil industry has so deformed the economy that most Venezuelans are no better off than their neighbors in non-industrialized countries. Although Venezuela's oil production has for many years been about three-quarters that of Texas, it has resulted in little of the secondary development of industry, the agriculture and culture which today characterize Texas. Or, in more general terms, the lowest stratum of Latin Americans is worse off today than at the end of World War II, although the intervening years have been marked by the biggest inflow of foreign capital and the greatest development of industry in the region's history.

I do not propose to spend a lot of time dragging skeletons out of closets or warming over the remains of old meals. However, I feel it is essential to understand the depth of the emotional gulf that separates us from the Latin American in our approach to the task which still remains to be performed, namely, the development of a viable economy in an area of this continent two and a half times the size of the United States. We tend to think, for example, that one of our greatest glories as a nation is that we rejected the temptation, when we had the power and when the international climate permitted, to occupy all or a large part of Latin America militarily and to extract the benefits which other great powers enjoyed as owners of colonies over the centuries. We point out that, even when circumstances forced or tempted us to move in this direction, we limited our occupation to the absolute minimum and withdrew as soon as our limited objectives had been assured.

The Latin American will not deny these obvious facts, but he will place them in a different perspective. Contrast the experience of India and China, he will say. The European powers exploited both these countries for two centuries with equal cynicism and with equal concern for their own advantage. They found that this advantage was best served in the case of India by occupying the country and creating a political and social structure geared to their needs. In China, on the contrary, they discovered by trial and error that they were able to develop a profitable trade while interfering only marginally and indirectly with the internal structure, that at most they needed control points, a Puerto Rico here, a Panama Canal there, a Guantanamo Bay somewhere else.

Now, the Latin American will ask, which of these two countries suffered the crueler and more irresponsible exploitation? When the system broke down in the middle of the twentieth century, India was vastly better off than China in terms of per capita income, levels of education, political sophistication, and ability to govern itself. India had the substructure, which (as Barbara Ward points out) makes it possible to plan and project a rate and direction of economic progress to a point of take-off and self-sustained growth. China was amorphous. Only human and material ruins remained and they had to be swept away before one could even begin to build a society, a perfect situation from the viewpoint of the Communists who had no problem of tearing down before starting their program.

I do not think it is likely that North Americans and Latin Americans will ever reach agreement on the degree of applicability of this comparison to the relations which have existed between themselves over the past century. I certainly do not pretend to have a definite answer. What I do know is that examples abound of individual United States and other foreign companies which have in specific situations abused their stranglehold over a segment of the economy of a Latin American country to their own benefit and in disregard of the general good of the country. I recall a spokesman of a major United States company boasting only a few years ago to a group of newsmen, of whom I was one, that his company had prevented the installation of a single new telephone in a major Latin American capital city for ten years until the government of that country agreed to the company's terms for a new agreement. As I see it, the rights and wrongs of the specific situation are immaterial. No foreign company should have that kind of power. Imagine a German or a Japanese company suspending the installation of new telephones in Washington, D. C., until Congress put through a law protecting its privileged status.

The example is extreme but not isolated. And I am not now thinking of such bitter critics as the distinguished Latin American author of the recently published *The Shark and the Sardines*. As conservative an observer as Ruby Hart Phillips, for some thirty years correspondent in Cuba for *The New York Times*, documents case after case in her book, *Cuba: Island of Paradox*. Written in the documentary style of the good, grey *Times*, where one wades through a column of circumstance to locate a fact, it describes events which she witnessed and reported at the time: the reckless lending of money by United States banks, secure in their knowledge that the marines would supervise collections and enforce foreclosures; the backing of Dictator Machado by United States companies which shared with him the unconscionable profits from the monopolies he awarded them.

More important than any effort to assess the theoretical rights and wrongs of the past is the exploration of the possibilities for an understanding for the future. Here, I think that things today look better than ever before. As a result of the unhappy personal experiences of Vice-President Nixon and President Eisenhower on their visits to Latin America, the Eisenhower administration began a reluctant re-evaluation of its previous extremely negative approach to hemisphere relations. By the end of 1960, it had reached some very important conclusions on the theoretical and philosophical level, conclusions which were eagerly adopted as a basis for action by the Kennedy administration, reduced to emotionally intelligible terms in the Alliance for Progress speech made by the new president in March 1961, and developed into a series of principles for common action by the Council of Foreign Ministers of the American States at Punta del Este, Uruguay, in August of the same year.

As I understand this program, it represents an acceptance by the United States of the Latin American viewpoint on inter-American relations, and it meets fully the criticisms of the past policies of foreign capital in Latin America which I have outlined above. Economic development is to be pursued at a rate of speed which will ensure a rapid and steady rise in living levels. Capital investment will be channeled into those areas in which it will achieve social as well as economic aims. The general welfare of the community will always take precedence over the individual benefit of the entrepreneur. In a word, the governments of the hemisphere will act individually and collectively to ensure in each country the utilization of the hemisphere's resources to achieve the kind of benefits which we in the United States have long enjoyed, thanks to the application of the same principles by our own business community under government supervision and regulation.

It is relatively easy to work out the theoretical problems, more complicated to apply them to concrete situations. The current development of the oil industry in Argentina may, however, be taken as an example. Under Perón, foreign oil companies were not allowed to explore, and in any case, the only basis on which they would have been willing to explore would have been under concessions giving them ownership of the oil and full freedom to exploit and sell it how and where they wished. The present Argentine government allowed the national oil company, the YPF, to bring in foreign companies under contract. This leaves ownership and control of the industry in national hands, ensuring development within the broad framework of national objectives and needs, while guaranteeing the technical know-how of the international companies. Under this arrangement, Argentina at the start of 1962 was producing 260,000 barrels of oil daily, enough to meet current domestic requirements. It was a small thing compared to Venezuela's actual production of 2,900,000 barrels daily at the same date and its potential of four million barrels daily, but for the country it was a much healthier foundation for national progress.

One of the first major tests of the new approach centers on a basic aspect of the international exchange of products, the terms of trade. The concept of terms of trade is theoretically simple but vastly complicated in practice. It is the price relationship between what you have to sell and what you seek to buy with the proceeds. If, for example, you can buy a tractor with the money you get by selling twenty bags of coffee, it does not matter whether you get $80, $100 or $120 a bag for the coffee, assuming that what you want to buy is a tractor. All that concerns you is that the prices of the two items move up and down in step. However, if the price for the coffee drops from $100 to $80 per bag, while the price of the tractor rises from $2,000 to $2,400, you now must sell thirty bags of coffee in order to buy the same tractor. The terms of trade have moved against you. Now you must either sell more coffee or make do with fewer tractors. And it is obvious that the additional quantity of coffee you can profitably sell at a given moment, even assuming you can produce it, is limited, because you will quickly saturate the market and break the price.

Latin America's dealings with the industrialized countries, especially the United States, have been greatly affected during recent years by a deterioration in the terms of trade. During World War II, rationing, price controls, bulk purchasing agreements and other devices maintained more or less the traditional relationships between the countries depending on the export of primary commodities, including the countries of Latin America, and the developed countries, including the United States. At war end, when controls were dropped, the prices of manufacturers rose rapidly, but in general terms, the prices of primary commodities, such as copper, tin, coffee, cacao, bananas, followed a similar upward trend, especially while the United States was engaged in stockpiling emergency supplies. During the year before the outbreak in Korea, the supply of primary commodities was beginning to exceed the effective demand, with a consequent easing of prices. However, the Korean War led to a major upsurge of demand and a new strengthening of prices, a condition which continued until about 1953, and for some commodities a little longer.

It is easy to criticize the way other people handle their affairs, and I know that much of the wealth that poured into Latin America in those years was spent wastefully, or ended up in the pockets of the ones who least needed it. But it is a fact of record, nevertheless, that the ten or twelve years following the end of World War II were the years of greatest economic progress in the history of Latin America. Gross national product increased at a rate so much faster than the rapid population growth as to provide an annual increase in real income per inhabitant substantially higher than that achieved by the United States during the same years, notwithstanding our lower rate of population increase. Gross national product rose 50 per cent between 1945 and 1954, while that of the United States rose 30 per cent, so that in spite of a demographic growth of 24 per cent, the per caput position improved considerably.

During the same years, the masses of the people in Latin America became aware of what was going on in the outside world and began to think that like miracles could happen for them. Sociologists have named this phenomenon the demonstration effect or the revolution of rising expectations. It reached the peasant and the slum dweller, making him not only ready but eager for change.

The new outlook reached the people via the modern mass media of communication, which have experienced a rapid development, but its emotional acceptance resulted, in my opinion, from the concurrent expansion of the economy, which enabled the man in the street to see progress and often to share in a little of its advantages. The actual development of the communications media is quite remarkable. For the visitor from the United States to any Latin American city, big or small, the quantities of printed materials on display are quite striking. Book stores and book stalls are everywhere, and they are laden down with masses of materials geared to every level of intelligence and literacy. They feature propaganda from Prague, Moscow and Peiping, as well as all sorts of offerings from the United States, including magazines like the Spanish edition of *Life*, which show in their pictorial and text content the extremely high living standards which the ordinary citizens of the United States enjoy. I am sorry to have to add that United

States publishers seem to have a near-monopoly on pornography and salacious magazines, and that they have achieved a wide distribution throughout the hemisphere for the same publications which disgrace many domestic news-stands.

One naturally finds less written material in the Latin American countryside, where illiteracy is widespread, but some newspapers and illustrated magazines reach even the remotest villages, and there is always somebody to read them aloud for curious neighbors. There are consequently few who do not have some kind of idea of what the outside world looks like and how it lives.

The radio, of course, is everywhere, and the development of the miniature transistor radio using regular flashlamp batteries has made it independent of electricity networks. I was amazed at a recent outdoor function one Sunday afternoon in a village in the Andes to find about ten or twelve of the local teen-agers carrying transistor radios slung round their necks. This was in itself simply a reflection of the impact of United States culture on the youth of the world, an impact also expressed in the haircuts and blue jeans of these *cocacolos*, as they are known in the local slang. But the use of the radio goes far beyond this group, and I think it is safe to say that it is the primary communications medium in underdeveloped countries, performing the function for which we rely on newspapers. Colombia alone has 120 radio transmitters, and other countries are equally saturated. The radio is used intensively to disseminate Communist ideas among the Indians of the Andean heartland of Ecuador, Peru and Bolivia. Catholics also use it, as in the famous radio schools of Colombia and the Institutes of Rural Education in Chile, and more recently Cardinal Cushing of Boston arranged the setting up of a series of transmitters in Peru and Bolivia to give a further dimension to his mission work in those countries. I shall return to these activities later.

The point I now want to make is that when the deterioration

in Latin America's terms of trade set in after 1953, it produced a reaction of anger and frustration at all levels of Latin American society. Governments found that they could not continue the development programs they had begun, because now they had fewer dollars from the sale of their exports. The small farmer found he could no longer buy schoolbooks or shoes for his children, because he was getting ten, twenty or fifty per cent less for his produce.

This decline in the value of exports occurred for reasons entirely outside the control of the countries affected, reasons totally unconnected with their economies. The average unit price for all Latin American exports was in 1959 only three-quarters of what it had been in 1951. For some commodities, the drop was far more drastic. The price of a leading grade of coffee, for example, fell by 46 per cent on the New York market between early 1954 and the end of 1958, and the downward trend continued at a slower tempo in subsequent years, so that the total decline registered by early 1962 was over 50 per cent.

It may be objected that the price of coffee was abnormally high, as it was in the year I selected as the starting year for my comparison, and that a survey of prices over a longer period would show a less abnormal relationship. Professional economists differ in their conclusions from the statistics available. It does, however, seem to be clear that the price of manufactured goods tends to fluctuate less than that of primary commodities, and that the unit price moves steadily upward. The case of a popular automobile manufactured in the United States seems typical. The basic retail list price for the two-door sedan was $640 in 1939, $1,002 in 1946, and $2,261 in 1961. The average worker engaged in manufacturing this car was not only better off at all times than the average worker engaged in production of primary commodities, but the gap between the two was wider at the end than at the beginning of the period.

Whatever may be the final conclusion about the long-term trend, there is no controversy about the effect of the tremendous short-term deterioration in the terms of Latin America's trade which set in during the middle 1950's. The trend toward rising standards of living and economic growth began to slow down in 1955, and by 1958 it had come close to a standstill. The negative impact was particularly severe in the agricultural sector, being reflected in actual decline in total production in 1960 as compared with previous years.

It should be noted, for critics of the United States have emphasized the point, that Latin Americans do not think of the deterioration of terms of trade so much as a problem between them and the industrialized countries as between them and one industrialized country, namely, the United States. During the period of deterioration, the United States has increased immensely its trade and financial stake in Latin America. United States exports to the region rose from $1 billion in 1940 to $5.2 billion in 1960; its imports from $900 million to $4.7 billion. Its direct private investments went from $2.8 billion in 1940 to $4.4 billion in 1950 and $8.4 billion in 1960, making it equivalent to 40 per cent of all United States private investment outside Canada and about three-quarters of all such investment in the less developed areas of the world. More than a third of the total was concentrated in oil, and less than a fifth was in manufacturing.

Increase in United States investments, however, does not involve a corresponding outflow of capital from the United States. What it represents principally is the high over-all level of success of the enterprises in which United States capital is invested, which enables them to build up capital values out of profits, in addition to returning capital home in the form of dividends. Thus, for South American countries which between them in 1960 represented nearly $6 billion of United States direct investment, the entire net increase over the previous year was accounted for by the plowing back of locally earned profits, the introduction of new United States capital in some countries being balanced by repatriation of capital from others. From the point of view of the economic stability of the host countries, these capital movements have a multiplier negative effect. Foreign capital is attracted by prosperity, flees when the economy is depressed, thereby accentuating the peaks and troughs.

The United States consumes nearly half of Latin America's primary products, and to all intents and purposes determines the world price for these products, determining it without any consideration of the cost of production. Each individual country is heavily dependent on exports of a few commodities, and the degree of dependence on a small number of commodities is growing. Twenty primary products accounted for nearly 80 per cent of Latin American exports in 1960, with petroleum, coffee and sugar in the lead. For the five leading products, the proportion of total exports is up from 37 per cent in 1937 to over 60 per cent in 1955–60. The share of coffee has doubled. Petroleum in normal years represents over 90 per cent of Venezuela's exports; coffee, 57 per cent those of Brazil; copper, 69 per cent those of Chile; and wool, 55 per cent those of Uruguay.

Between 1937 and 1957, the volume of world exports was up 77 per cent, but the volume of Latin American exports was up only 18 per cent. Omitting petroleum, there was an actual decline. Between the late 1920's and the mid-1950's, Latin America suffered a decline in its share of world commerce in products which in 1955–57 constituted more than 75 per cent of its exports.

In addition to these long-term adverse trends, foreign exchange earnings have been highly variable on a year-to-year basis. Uruguay's exchange earnings, for example, declined nearly one half between 1956 and 1957, and well over a half between 1956 and

1959. Export prices of Uruguayan wool were in 1959 at only 35 per cent of the 1951 level, though they recovered to about 47 per cent of that level in 1960. This is as if our automobile's price had slipped from $1,002 to $350 in 1959 and $470 in 1960, though in fact in this last named year we were selling it for $2,250.

The impact on the economy of such fluctuations in export prices is vastly greater than would be the case in the United States. Here, the economy depends primarily on the domestic market, with only a small percentage of marketed products destined for export. In many Latin American countries, the situation is reversed. The domestic market is marginal, and export prices constitute the determining factor. We can defend our prices against major pressures. During the United States recession of 1958, the steel industry cut production to 50 per cent of capacity rather than lower prices. The Latin Americans can exert only marginal control over export prices, and when they attempt to do even this, we immediately scream monopoly and market rigging.

Simultaneously with, and closely connected to the deterioration in the terms of trade, many countries experienced runaway inflation and drastic increases in the cost of living. Taking a figure of 100 for December 1953, the cost of living index in December 1960 stood at 945 in Chile, 622 in Argentina, 485 in Brazil, 358 in Uruguay, and more than 3,500 in Bolivia.

It is against this background that one must evaluate the deterioration in relations between the United States and Latin America during recent years. There is no doubt that first the Communists and subsequently also the Castroites manipulated and distorted the events to poison the public mind against the United States. But it is equally true that they had real grievances to exploit. And when the initial United States reaction was to wash its hands and insist that it could not interfere with the operation of the economic laws, as it was, many Latin Americans felt with considerable justification that the aid being given simultaneously by the United States to build their economies was a pharisaical gesture, since its amount was far less than what these economies were losing each year through the deterioration of the terms of trade.

All of this leads to the ultimate question. What concretely does Latin America expect of the United States? What seems to emerge from an evaluation of the conflicting specific reactions is that whatever the United States does, whether it gives, lends, invests or withdraws, it is always found blameworthy. It can't win. During the past thirty years, it has made several efforts to work out new relationships. It has done so under a variety of favorable conditions: the advantage of geographic proximity, the generosity of the United States taxpayer, the knowledge among Latin Americans of the material success of the United States and their admiration for this material success. The results have been at best far less spectacular than the means, while during the same period the Communists without any of the advantages just named have achieved big results with far less effort.

I think that one reason for the disappointing results is that the people of the United States do not understand what makes their own way of life a success. They want to sell Latin America what they think is the entire package: high taxation, parliamentary democracy, religious plurality, not recognizing that other elements balance and give positive content to these factors, and in particular that they work in the United States because they are subject to social and political controls, from the anti-monopoly legislation to farm parity.

Another reason militating against progress is that the United States partner wants to run the show. The private investor insists on control in each country, especially if his investment is part of an international chain of similar enterprises. The local partner is concerned with only his part and is entirely dependent on its success. The United States partner has different interests. It may suit him to make a loss in one country in a given year, perhaps to benefit his business elsewhere, perhaps for United States tax considerations.

Basically, the man in the Latin American street believes that the United States interests, and foreign business interests in general, make decisions without regard for their impact on the economy of the country affected. And when he passes this judgment, he is not far wide of the mark, for the United States businessman calls himself and is a capitalist, and a characteristic of capitalism is the profit motive.

The dilemma has been resolved in practice inside developed capitalistic countries like the United States by two sets of controls. One set is economic in its nature. The capitalist with a major investment in a given market recognizes that, to protect his investment, he must conduct his business in that market in such a way as to maintain the economic soundness not only of his business but of the market as well, a principle which one of our leading capitalists attempted to express a few years back in a phrase that was close to the mark though politically unfortunate: what's good for General Motors is good for the country.

The second set of controls on capitalism in developed countries is primarily political, consisting of the curbs on monopolies, the supervision of public service companies, the organization of trades unions, and the other elements to which I referred a little while back. I am sure that Latin America will opt for capitalism, if once it is exposed to a capitalism which works for it in the way in which United States capitalism works for the United States. The controls established by the Mexican revolution over the operation of foreign capital in Mexico, as I pointed out earlier, were designed to provide the guarantees for the public of Mexico which the United States public rightly demands for itself at home. The recent history of the Mexican economy shows that foreign capital can operate profitably within such controls. But it doesn't like them and continues to oppose them elsewhere in Latin America. In this respect, it is very like the traditional Latin American ruling classes. It finds things good the way they are, and it is too shortsighted to recognize that they could be better, and certainly far more stable, if it would throw its weight on the side of progress.

The semantic and emotional elements in this misunderstanding have to be recognized. We in the United States are deeply and properly committed to the economic system that works for us, and which we are accustomed to call capitalism. But the word has a very different meaning elsewhere, even for people who cannot be suspected of Communist leanings. "As far removed from Christianity as Communism itself," is the comment recently made by Archbishop Juan Landazuri, O.F.M., of Lima, Peru, who added, "The Church condemns capitalism and also the miserable situation to which it has led innumerable workers."

The archbishop did not, of course, mean to denounce private ownership, free enterprise, or fair profits. He is opposed simply to those aspects of capitalism which the American conscience has rejected by the laws we have enacted. Like us, he is opposed to monopolies which can strangle the country and do away with the little man, to the idea that government should never use a subsidy to help the farmer, a loan to the small homeowner, or a social security system in favor of the general public.

It will be evident that we are here faced with a problem which is moral as well as economic, and that what ultimately is being called for is the recognition of the existence of a zone of mutual responsibility wider than national boundaries, implying the broadening of the concept of citizenship, with its rights and obligations, to embrace the hemisphere. That a body of informed opinion is prepared to recognize the need for this drastic step is evident from the hemispheric response to President Kennedy's Alliance for Progress proposals, and for the concrete form in which they were defined at the Punta del Este conference. For example, to return to the specific problem of terms of trade just discussed, the signatories of the Final Declaration, including the United States, put themselves on record as recognizing that the economic development of Latin America requires "the correction of the secular deterioration" in the terms of trade.

To achieve the objectives of the Alliance for Progress will require, among other things, a huge capital investment in Latin America during the coming decade. Since population is increasing at a rate of about 2.5 per cent per annum, output of goods and services must increase at the same rate simply to prevent a deterioration. To effect on top of this an acceptable improvement in per capita living standards will require an over-all growth rate of 5 to 6 per cent per annum. As a rule of thumb, economists say that underdeveloped countries must invest an amount equal to about 4 per cent of the goods and services produced in order to increase the rate of output by 1 per cent. For a 5 to 6 per cent increase, accordingly, investment must equal twenty to twenty-five per cent of the gross national product.

Since current total value of all goods and services produced in Latin America is in the neighborhood of $70–75 billion, capital investment of about $18 billion annually will be needed to raise the national income by the required 5 to 6 per cent. The magnitude of this task becomes apparent when it is recalled that the World Bank loaned Latin American countries a grand total of $1,441 million between 1948 and 1962, and that $500 million mentioned by President Kennedy as a first installment in his Alliance for Progress speech and subsequently voted by Congress represents only about 3 per cent of the amount needed in a single year.

Former President Kubitschek of Brazil was more realistic when in 1958 he put forward his Operation Pan America, forerunner of the Alliance. While he did not fix a figure officially, his advisers indicated that it would take up to $40 billion in foreign loans, investments and grants to double the per capita income of Latin Americans in the next ten to fifteen years. Apparently, United States thinking is getting nearer this viewpoint, for in the Declaration to the Peoples of America signed at the Punta del Este Conference in August 1961, the United States not only pledged its efforts to supply financial and technical cooperation in order to achieve the aims of the Alliance for Progress, but undertook to provide a major part "of the minimum of twenty billion dollars, principally in public funds, which Latin America will require over the next ten years from all external sources in order to supplement its own efforts."

It is not my purpose or intention to present a detailed blueprint of the proposed development process, but I think it is possible to sketch rapidly some outlines capable of dispelling widely held misunderstandings.

The purpose of international aid as conceived today by world opinion and formulated by the United Nations and other international organizations supported by the United States is to help project the less developed countries forward to the take-off point for self-sustained economic growth, after which they will be able to continue to advance under their own power in the kind of controlled chain reaction which characterizes the economy of the United States and other developed countries. Since Latin America has a favorable relationship of population to resources, a relatively long period of political stability, an absence of major cultural barriers, and a similarity of institutions to those of the industrialized countries, more rapid and dramatic results can be anticipated from international aid than in the case of Asia or Africa.

The role of outside capital, whether public or private, can never be more than marginal in the development process. Latin Americans themselves are already investing annually about 15 per cent of their gross national product, and foreign sources are contributing a further 2 to 3 per cent. A few extra percentage points would make a difference out of all proportion to the sums involved, and this is what the current excitement is about. We are near the critical moment, and a small rise in temperature would make the reaction self-sustaining. Most of the additional investment, moreover, must—like most of current investment—come from internal savings, and in consequence the problem is not simply one of loans or grants, as it tends to become in discussion in the United States, but rather a total readjustment of both internal and external economic factors to restore the kind of situation that existed between 1945 and 1955, namely inflows or accumulations of substantial quantities of capital, favorable trade terms, broadening world and domestic markets, distinct improvements in productivity.

Absence of any one of these interrelated factors can vitiate the entire program. No net benefit, for example, results from pumping in stopgap foreign capital, if it is merely replacing domestic capital stashed away in Switzerland or the United States by wealthy people who fear unrest. Nor will aid dollars help to build industry and streamline agriculture, unless a reordering of social conditions spreads purchasing power among the masses so that they can buy the additional food and manufactures. For such reasons, apart from any other considerations of justice, equity or politics, the social aspects of the Alliance for Progress constitute an integral part of the package.

For twenty years, the United States has been the main source of foreign capital for Latin America, and several lending agencies, each with a specific purpose, have been formed to help finance economic development and the international movement of goods and services. All these agencies encourage private investment, and some of them draw part of their capital from private sources.

The Export-Import Bank, an independent agency of the United States Government, provides credits in dollars to buy United States goods and services. Bank credits authorized for Latin America during its first twenty-five years up to 1960 exceed $4 billion. During 1961, it approved $490 million in loans and guarantee transactions. The purpose of this institution, however, is not to help develop Latin America but to aid United States exporters, and while it has been useful, many Latin Americans feel that the same credit combined with freedom to utilize it in the open market would mean much more. Restriction of the credit means that the Latin American who avails himself of it must buy United States goods or services, even if something less expensive or better geared to his needs is obtainable elsewhere.

The Development Loan Fund, also a U. S. government corporation, established in 1957, makes dollar loans which in certain circumstances can be repaid in foreign currencies. Its purpose is to finance projects designed to increase the productive capacity and economic resources of underdeveloped countries. Loans to Latin America by mid-1960 amounted to $94.4 million. Some additional development financing is provided by the International Cooperation Administration, a semi-autonomous agency within the Department of State, although its main function is to train foreign personnel, provide special assistance to foreign governments with balance of payments or budgetary problems, and to help in disasters. It administers the Public Law 480 programs which make local currencies available from the sale of surplus United States agricultural commodities abroad.

The World Bank, an international agency which receives a major part of its funds from the United States, lends to member governments, or to borrowers guaranteed by member governments, for productive projects for which private capital is not available on reasonable terms. By 1962, it has authorized loans in Latin America exceeding $1.4 billion for such projects as reconstruction, electric power, transportation, communications, agriculture and forestry, industry and general development. The relatively low level of its impact emerges when it is noted that loans to all Latin America in the second half of 1961 totaled only $83 million.

Two affiliates of the World Bank have recently been created to extend its area of help, the International Finance Corporation in 1956, and the International Development Association in 1960. The former makes investments in productive private enterprises in member countries without the guarantee of repayment by the government. Up to March 1962, it lent $43 million to private companies in Latin America, three-quarters of its total operation. The latter is designed to finance economic development on terms more flexible and bearing less heavily on the balance of payments of recipient countries than ordinary loans. It is starting its operations with a fund of one billion dollars, of which the United States has subscribed nearly a third.

For many years Latin American economists and planners had been complaining that none of these institutions corresponded fully to their needs. Direction and policy, they contended, were remote from the realities and sentiments of the Latin American scene. Toward the end of 1960, finally, the United States bowed to their insistence and reluctantly agreed to join with them in an Inter-American Development Bank to provide financial and technical assistance for the economic development of the Americas. All member countries of the Organization of American States except Cuba have joined in this first regional bank and are scheduled to subscribe just under a billion dollars for its operations, the United States contribution being $450 million. In June 1961, this bank assumed responsibility for administering a $394 million Social Progress Trust Fund established by the United States as one of the first steps for the Alliance for Progress. By April 1962 it had granted a hundred loans for a total of $428 million, a little more than half the money coming from the Social Progress Trust Fund.

The number of organizations is perhaps more impressive than the amount of their contribution, which represents only a small percentage of what is needed. Nevertheless, these institutions constitute an important part of the entire Latin American picture. If only on a pilot scale, they are operating entities, with the know-how and facilities for rapid expansion when the international community decides to move ahead. They are an important part of the preparation for progress.

8

+ — + — *Religion's Primal Role*

PROBABLY NO PART OF THE UNITED States image of Latin America is more confused or more distorted than its concept of the place and function of the Catholic Church in Latin American society.

Many elements have combined to create this picture. The Black Legend about Spain and Spain's Catholicism in Anglo-Saxon cultures since the Reformation was projected in attitudes toward Spain's former possessions. Protestant missionaries from the United States played a major part in the last century in "discovering" Latin America and interpreting it back home. Few Catholic historians and scholars have specialized in the area, and most of these concern themselves mainly with a Catholic audience. The proportion of United States Catholics specializing in Latin American trade, commerce, industry or government service is considerably lower than the statistical proportion of Catholics in the general population. North Americans in the Latin American field meet relatively few practicing Catholics among their Latin American counterparts, and frequently those who profess Catholicism not only reveal slight knowledge of their religion but combine their ignorance with anticlerical attitudes and a low opinion of the clergy.

The Church remains, nevertheless, the all-pervading and all-influencing reality of Latin American history. Attempts to evaluate the past, present, or future of the hemisphere without taking it into account are even less realistic than it would be to interpret the United States without reference to the Puritan tradition of a small but long dominant segment of our population. The recent history of Mexico offers a striking example of this fact. Here, all the negative factors combined to ensure the destruction of the Church as an institution and a social reality. Yet, as noted earlier, it has emerged a winner in its proper sphere from the revolutionary turmoil. The observer at the shrine of Our Lady of Guadalupe outside Mexico City any day of the week immediately recognizes that such is the case. He may develop any one of a number of theories to explain the fact, but he will not be tempted to deny it.

It may be appropriate to review the historical background, many elements of which have already been noted in different contexts. Spanish government policy from the time of the discovery on gave primary emphasis to converting the inhabitants of the New World to Christianity, and almost from the start a contest developed between the adventurers anxious to exploit the Indians for their own benefit and the clergy entrusted with civilizing and christianizing them. In the first period of the Conquest, the Church achieved notable success in laying solid foundations for its task. Among the important institutions it developed was the encomienda, a mis-

sion center around which the Indians were grouped in order to
be taught not only the faith but the intellectual and material elements of civilized life. This system reached a high level of success
in the south-center of South America, in what is now northern
Argentina, Paraguay and Bolivia.

This success was achieved not by force of arms but by the action of missionaries over whom the civil power exercised little or
no control. In 1609, the Jesuits undertook to civilize the Indians
in Paraguay, and they continued their work there for 158 years, until they were expelled in 1767.

During this time, they established in Paraguay alone 32 "Reductions," establishments operated on the basis of a kind of paternalistic socialism. They persuaded the Indians to come out of
the forests and establish towns where they built magnificent
churches, discovered and utilized unsuspected talents of the natives as masons, stoneworkers, woodworkers, sculptors and painters.
Education of the Indians progressed so rapidly that many of them
acquired a sound classical training. The first settlements in the
north had to be abandoned because of constant attacks from Brazil, and the Jesuits finally settled in the Province of Misiones, so
that part of their area of operation was beyond what is now the
frontier of Argentina. After the expulsion of the Jesuits, their work
gradually disappeared. The Indians left the towns and were reduced to the condition of peons under other masters. Most of the
great churches and the other buildings have fallen into ruin or
been destroyed. However, even today the effect of this civilizing
work remains. For example, Paraguayans are bilingual, speaking
both Spanish and Guaraní, a language more highly developed
than any of the other Indian tongues of the continent. The people
have a pride both in their language and in the customs and traditions of their ancestors, so that they have in fact formed a distinctive culture combining desirable elements of the indigenous

and of the imported way of life. If the noble experiment had been allowed to develop according to its own rhythm, it might have meant a very different writing of the subsequent history of South America.

Unfortunately, this was not to be. The adventurers were stronger than the Church, and they transformed the encomiendas into privately-owned haciendas in which the Indians were made the serfs of the landowners. The downgrading of the Church was facilitated and speeded by events in Europe. Most of the mission effort was entrusted to the religious orders, among whom the Jesuits were particularly important. A power struggle in Europe resulted in the expulsion of the Jesuits from the Portuguese dominions in 1755 and from those of Spain twelve years later, leaving a vacuum in Latin America which was never filled. Meanwhile, a shocking decline in observance had set in among many of the other religious orders. Various reasons are offered for this evolution of the Spanish Church in the Indies from evangelical purity to corrupt refinement, but the fact cannot be called into question, being thoroughly documented by such trustworthy historians as Salvador de Madariaga in his *The Rise of the Spanish American Empire*.

The religious decline was accelerated half a century later by the events leading to the emancipation of the American colonies. For reasons unconnected with the conditions of the New World, Rome had given Spain and Portugal the so-called *patronato*, or right to name all bishops in their dominions, a privilege which made religious life in the colonies excessively dependent on Madrid and Lisbon. When the political clash came, most of the bishops sided with Spain, not only because they were Spaniards but because their careers depended on the royal favor. In justice to them, it must be recalled that the liberation party drew much of its inspiration from the revolutionary movements of contemporary

Europe, violently anticlerical, often anti-religious. The triumph of
the Revolution brought for these bishops exile or deposition.
Many of the lower clergy also were Spaniards, and even when not
directly affected by the change, they suffered from the widened gap
between them and the new rulers.

Spain was still the world's leading Catholic power, and for a
long time it was far from clear whether the separation of the
American possessions was going to be permanent or not. In any
case, Spain's influence was able to delay papal recognition of the
new states, and since these latter claimed to enjoy by inheritance
all privileges formerly exercised by Spain, including the *patronato*,
the situation grew progressively worse. By 1829, only ten of 29
dioceses had bishops, and many seminaries had been forcibly
closed. For a generation or more, the confusion continued. Even
after new arrangements, sometimes formal, sometimes informal,
were made to regularize Church-State relations and permit the appointment of bishops, the Church never fully recovered, not even
in the countries in which things worked out most favorably for it.

Many Spanish priests had returned to Europe, and it was for a
long time difficult or impossible to bring replacements. Church
discipline became more relaxed. Vocations declined. State support of seminaries and other educational institutions was withdrawn or reduced, and the poverty of the people combined with
the absence of any tradition of popular financial support for religious activities prevented the development of a dynamic system
of Church-directed schools.

From there on, it seemed that the only direction in which the
Church could go was down. In many of the newly formed States, it
allied itself with the conservative groups, people who more or less
enthusiastically accepted the fact of political emancipation, but
who definitely wanted no accompanying social change. By the
early part of the twentieth century, the conclusion appeared in-

escapable that the Catholic Church's role in Latin America was bound to become progressively less. All over the world, the trend of public life was toward a separation of the ecclesiastical and civil powers, with a reduction or elimination of religious controls not only in politics but in the fields of charity, education and social work. The conservative groups on whom the Church had relied in Latin America to save her from this fate were themselves clearly on the wane, and most likely would carry her along with them into the grave on whose brink they were tottering.

Even in the strictly spiritual field, in which a proper function might be recognized for the Church, many observers were doubtful regarding her chances of survival. The educated urban classes had become emotionally divorced from her. Several generations of secular and anticlerical education had left them religiously illiterate. Their lived ideology was "liberal" and French rather than Catholic and Spanish. In so far as they felt the need for transcendental solutions, they believed they could find them in philosophy or science.

The masses, both urban and rural, were equally devoid of any intellectual basis for their traditional emotional attachment to their faith, and such scanty and irregular practice of their religion as they retained was heavily overlain with superstitions and pagan survivals. The predominantly rural structure and static nature of society had permitted the transmission of the faith from father to son, even without priests, but urbanization would accelerate the loss and eliminate the surviving religious practices. The mass media of communication, especially radio, cinema and television, were rapidly spreading among them the ideology lived by the intellectuals. Many in the cities were undergoing the proletarization which had earlier affected the urban masses in France and elsewhere, a process that seemed to be preparing the way for the onset of Marxism.

During these same years, nevertheless, currents were developing below the surface which finally have changed the direction of the Church's movement and instilled a new dynamism into her efforts. Intellectual movements began to stir, inspired by the neo-Thomism which had been inaugurated in Europe before the turn of the century. The impact of the social encyclicals of Leo XIII and his successors finally produced an echo among Catholic sociologists in Latin America. The world upheaval of World War II forced a new evaluation of social realities. Painfully but honorably, the Church has come to recognize, in one country after another, that the teaching of Christ in today's circumstances leaves it with no alternative other than to support and encourage the desires of the masses for the more human conditions of life which are every man's birthright and which man's new mastery of the material world has made technically possible.

For those who do not stop to figure out how the Church operates, this process has created considerable confusion. It is not possible to point to any sensational moment or event in Latin America, any sudden reversal of policy, any ousting or downgrading of recalcitrant holdouts. What occurs is a gradual change of emphasis, adjusted to local conditions and needs. The new bishop is more favorably disposed to trades union organization than his predecessor. He introduces a new textbook on social problems in his seminary. He invites a missionary society to develop a parish in a hitherto ignored slum. Only by studying an accumulation of incidents can one recognize the presence of a trend.

If one event must be singled out as the formal beginning of the new era in the Church in Latin America, I like to think that it was a meeting which opened on the last day of 1945 at the Colegio de Belén, Havana, Cuba, which it was my privilege to attend. The seminar was composed of representatives chosen by the Catholic hierarchy of each nation and territory of the American continent,

and we had come to inform each other and be informed of the social problems of the Americas, as a prelude to developing common policies. I was then editor of a daily newspaper in a small
Caribbean island, and my modest contribution to the proceedings
was an outline of its racial problems.

By coincidence, history was being made in other terms at the
Colegio de Belén at the same moment. Were it not for the long
vacation, we might have met in the corridors a student who was
later to loom large in American affairs, a beardless youth named
Fidel Castro. Both the famed high school and equally famed ob-
servatory have long since been seized by his Communist regime.

For several days, I listened with fascination to the reports given
by the delegates from each country on the major problems affecting society in their country and the programs or intentions for dealing with them. Leaving aside the United States and Canada, there
was a broad similarity in the reports. They dwelt on illiteracy, excessive concentration of land in big holdings (*latifundismo*), excessive fragmentation of land in uneconomically small holdings
(*minifundismo*), socio-racial handicaps of Indians and Negroes,
lack of worker organizations or the defects of those that existed.
Since more than half the delegates were priests, and since the
seminar's professed purpose was to develop programs based on
Catholic social teachings, it is understandable that there was also
considerable discussion of matters of direct concern to the Church,
such as the fewness of vocations and the sacristy-centeredness of
Church activities.

What seems strange to me now is that I recall little reference to
Communist penetration of Latin America or to population pressures. I do not mean that the subjects were not mentioned. Communism was very much alive in the politics of several countries,
because the still fresh wartime alliance with Russia had given legal-
ity and prestige to local Communist leaders. But mostly everyone

dismissed them as amiable faddists. Whatever else might change, certain immutable facts remained. And one of these was that Latin Americans were Catholics. According to them, neither Protestantism nor Communism nor any other denial of the Faith need be feared, to say nothing of the geo-strategic impossibility of a Communist government on this continent.

As for population, it must be remembered that the number of Latin Americans in 1945 was less than half what it is today. Many countries were looking forward to a postwar upsurge of immigration from Europe to stimulate economic expansion. If there were pressures on the resources of some islands and one or other Central American republic, so much empty space existed within easy reach that nobody got over-excited.

Several things which did then seem strange to me have become today less remarkable, not because they are not significant, but because I have got used to them. Perhaps I should mention first the almost complete absence of reported progress with solutions to the problems that were presented, or even of agreement as to what solutions were called for. What this means is that it is only since World War II that the Catholic Church in Latin America has begun to feel serious concern about the social system, or at least to feel that it could do something about it. This concern, of course, reflected a tremendous change in mental attitudes, and I think great credit is due to a few American priests who had long been quietly urging their Latin American colleagues to wake up. Two of these, Father John LaFarge, S.J., editor of *America*, and Father Raymond McGowan, head of NCWC's Social Action Department, were main architects of the seminar at the Colegio de Belén.

Another thing that struck me was the extraordinary range of social attitudes reflected by the delegates. Many had a personal commitment to social justice and an eagerness to see change, even when they felt that the dead weight of powerful tradition made their position hopeless. Others were hesitant to draw conclusions that seemed to them revolutionary from the principles they could not deny. A minority, though a vocal one, saw nothing shameful in things as they were, apparently felt no discomfort in defending a system that provided human conditions of life and culture for only a privileged few. These were mostly from countries in which the Church still enjoyed, or still hoped to recover, the two-edged benefit of state subsidization of a clerical establishment.

The most publicized, if not the most important, of the changes that have since become apparent in the programs and attitudes of the Catholic Church in Latin America, is in its relations with dictators. During the 1950's, the hierarchies of four separate countries played an important part by their public statements in the overthrow of four of the hemisphere's most notorious dictators: Perón in Argentina, Rojas Pinilla in Colombia, Pérez Jiménez in Venezuela, and Batista in Cuba. In each case, the effect of the stand was to range the Church publicly with groups seeking political liberty and social reform with whom, even twenty-five years earlier, cooperation would have been unimaginable.

A more significant development was the creation in 1955 of the Latin American Bishops' Council, a hemisphere organization with obvious parallels to the National Catholic Welfare Conference through which the bishops of the United States develop common policies and coordinate action on education, social affairs, information, youth, and other matters. The secretariat of the Bishops' Council in Bogotá, Colombia, has five sections dealing, respectively, with the preservation of the faith; the clergy and religious institutes; education and youth; lay apostolate; social action and welfare.

The pastoral renewal in Latin America can be traced to two sources, an internal revival within the countries concerned, and greater help from the Church in Europe and the United States. Among the elements characterizing the movement is a big increase in vocations designed to lessen the dependence on outside priests. The diocese of Tulancingo in Mexico, for example, succeeded in raising the number of priests ordained for the diocese so substantially in a period of fifteen years as to make itself almost independent of outside help. Previously it had supplied only half its needs. For all of Mexico, the number of ordinations annually has grown to approximately 250, still only equivalent to 4 per cent of the country's total priests, but at least ensuring replacements for those who die or retire. Mexico has set up a splendid record with the establishment of several major seminaries, such as that at Guadalajara, where more than a thousand candidates are being trained. In these respects, Mexico is far ahead of most Latin American countries, but in all of them the development of an indigenous clergy is progressing. Colombia has improved the ratio of its priests in twenty years from one for 6,200 Catholics to one for 3,800. Allowing for increased population, this represented an actual doubling of the number of priests. The institutional development which has contributed most to this progress in Colombia is an increase in the number of minor seminaries. Of the thirty-four operating in 1962, twenty had been opened since 1938, and during the same period, twelve so-called apostolic schools have been established. They feed additional candidates into the country's seventeen major seminaries, the combined enrollment in which has now gone above one thousand. Also noteworthy has been the creation of a seminary for late vocations, which opened with 14 candidates in 1959, grew to 44 in 1960, and more than a hundred in 1961.

A shortage of priests is still one of the most fundamental problems of the Church in Latin America. For the whole of South America, there are 11,897 diocesan and 15,846 religious priests, a total of 27,743 priests, according to the 1960 edition of *Basic Ec-*

clesiastical Statistics for Latin America. They serve 126 million
Catholics spread over an area of more than seven million square
miles. This gives one priest for each 4,550 Catholics, and a population density of 18.9 persons per square mile, which means an
average of 240 square miles of territory for each priest to take
care of.

The Central American and Mexican area has 5,520 diocesan
and 2,152 religious priests, a total of 7,672. They serve forty million
Catholics who inhabit almost a million square miles of territory,
giving one priest for 5,200 Catholics and a population density of
41.8 per square mile. A priest in the Central American and Mexican area would normally have charge of an area half the size allo-
cated to his colleague in South America.

In the Caribbean, the population density is greater, 200 per
square mile, but there are even fewer priests, one for every 5,850
Catholics. In all, there are 841 diocesan and 1,664 religious priests,
a total of 2,505, and they serve nearly fifteen million Catholics in
an area of 92,000 square miles.

These figures assume greater meaning by noting that Europe has
one priest for 900 Catholics, Asia one priest for 1,300 Catholics,
and Africa one priest for 1,400 Catholics. The population density
is also meaningful. More than half of Latin America is still rural,
with people spread out over vast areas, often mountainous,
often trackless. No matter how active a priest is, he can reach few
of his parishioners in the course of a week's or a month's work. In
the United States, by way of contrast, some 80 per cent of Catholics are concentrated in urban areas within easy reach of a parish
church. There is an average of one priest for 750 Catholics. Even
for the Catholics living in the big cities of Latin America, the dis-
proportion between the number of faithful and the number of
priests is so great as to prevent effective impact. Estimates made
during the 1950's showed that Buenos Aires averaged 27,000 Catho-

lics and three priests per parish; Havana, 60,000 Catholics and two priests. It will be appreciated that not all priests are available for parish work. Some teach in seminaries, colleges or high schools, others are administrators, are engaged in higher studies, or are retired. In Colombia, for example, in 1960 only two-thirds of the country's 2,339 diocesan priests and one fourth of its 1,849 religious priests worked as pastors or assistant pastors. This meant that, while Colombia had one priest for every 3,810 Catholics, each priest engaged in parish work had an average of 7,429 Catholic parishioners to care for.

Recently it was my good fortune to visit a parish in Peru which had long lacked a resident priest, and where a new pastor is now trying to develop once more a sense of community and the practices of religion. A brief description will both show some of the general problems and reveal the new spirit spreading in the Church.

The parish is located in a valley of the Andes mountains not far from Lima. While its limits are somewhat vaguely defined, it stretches twenty or more miles along the valley, and its effective width is defined by the contours of the mountains on each side, which in parts narrow to a few miles, elsewhere spread out into minor valleys where there are villages or smaller groups of houses. Most of the land is concentrated in a few estates, operated in the traditional manner of the hacienda. One of these alone stretches fourteen miles along the valley. Hacienda workers are clustered in a compound around the estate house, where the owner comes occasionally for weekends or a change of air from his palatial home in Lima. A small chapel attached to the house is available to the pastor to say Mass and administer the sacraments, whenever he can get there. Eight or nine miles away is a sleepy village, a hollow square of squat houses constructed by the Spaniards hundreds of years ago. The dilapidated church boasts a bell cast in 1720, and little more. The village lacks electricity, a telephone, a doctor. There is no rectory, nor any kind of lodginghouse in which the priest could spend a night.

Some miles further on lies another hacienda with its group of adjoining hovels clustered in a compound. To the north, hidden by a jutting flank of the mountain, is yet another small village. Wherever the pastor goes, he is greeted with moving affection by young and old. Everyone asks him when is he coming to spend a long period with them. He promises to do his best, but what does that mean? The poverty of the people is such that no economic basis exists in any of these centers of population for a rectory and parish activities. And no matter which of them he selects, he is many hours away from all the others, even by jeep. The jeep, of course, is something new, and the pastor has one only because it was contributed by well-wishers in the United States. Previously, travel was by horse or mule. For an emergency, the message was brought by a runner, and then the priest spent perhaps a whole day traveling, according to distance. In such circumstances, even such basic Christian practices as administration of the last rites for the dying were almost always out of the question.

For the moment, the pastor's direct efforts for these scattered parishioners cannot go much beyond visiting the centers in turn on Sundays to say Mass and to catechize and administer the sacraments. To come during the week ordinarily achieves little, since the people are away all day in the fields.

This particular pastor, however, has a quite different projection for the future. At the lower end of the parish, closest to Lima, a home construction development has begun for middle-class people from the overflowing city. The law in Peru prescribes that a housing center must provide not only roads and sewers but space for a parish center. Only the land is given, but this is a start. The new community will consist of people with some drive, some education, open to change, living in a money economy, and with some capital of their own. They can provide an economic basis for a parish which will one day have its own church, rectory, hall, clinic and school.

With such a dynamic parish center, the pastor can see ways of bringing substantial spiritual help to the impoverished Indians in the valley and along the slopes of the mountains. He sees an assistant who will enable him to hang out the shingle that is beginning to mark the more progressive parishes, a simple sign notifying the passer-by that a priest is on call at all hours of the day and night. He sees in each isolated village and compound an Indian catechist trained to teach the truths of religion and paid a living wage for his work, a man to lead prayer in the priest's absence and to prepare for religious functions ahead of his arrival. He sees a small radio transmitter in each catechist's home to summon the priest in an emergency, especially in the great emergency for which each must today prepare without the whispered absolution or the anointing with holy oils.

The situation I have described is far from extreme. The climate is dry and healthy, and the proximity to a big city ensures for the priest the availability of congenial intellectual companionship, as well as assurance of help in sickness or other emergency. Far other are the circumstances high on the plateaus of the Andean heartland, at altitudes above sea level of ten to fifteen thousand feet, or deep in the steaming jungles of the Amazonian hinterland east of the mountains. Physical effort is exhausting, and the isolation is terrifying. Even under favorable conditions, many days' travel may be necessary simply to reach the next priest or a doctor. In the rainy season, when trails are washed out, help may be weeks away. Here, the Argentine saying that distance kills has full validity. For if the solitude which one seeks raises the soul, the remoteness which isolates a man breaks the spirit. And these distances are hard to grasp. Brazil alone is bigger than the continental United States. Argentina is four times the size of Texas; all of Europe outside Russia could fit in it. The average parish in the Argentine diocese of Viedma is 5,735 square miles in extent, which is bigger than the state of Connecticut, and its 15,500 Catholics are scattered at an average density of fewer than three per square mile. Population density in another Argentine diocese, Comodoro Rivadavia, is only slightly more than one per square mile, and its average parish has 14,000 spread over an area bigger than two of Viedma's parishes. In all of Argentina, there are only 1,300 parishes for a Catholic population of 20,000,000, whereas we here in the United States have nearly 17,000 parishes for a Catholic population of about 43,000,000. Add to this the inadequacy of roads, railroads, and other means of communication, and you can see that the most zealous and energetic pastor can hope to reach in any meaningful way only a small minority of his parishioners.

A strange, if convenient, myth has achieved wide acceptance about these forgotten people living idyllically far from the pressures and temptations of civilization. Rousseau's imaginative evocation of the noble savage lingers in the mind when they are mentioned. How different is the reality emerges from a study of the family recently conducted under Catholic auspices in Colombia. It distinguished three zones in the country: a monogamous zone, a polygamous zone, and an intermediate zone.

In the first, the region of Antioquia, Caldas and part of Chocó, there is a more developed middle class, and here Catholic marriage is the rule, especially in this class. Cohabitation without marriage does not exceed 10 per cent. At the other extreme, on the coast and in the river and mining areas, about 20 per cent of unions are based on Catholic marriage. Some of the others are free but stable, what is called faithful concubinage, with the offspring considered legitimate. But the normal type is unstable, based on cultural values, such as virility, wealth and prestige. A man is considered well off if he has several women working for him, and in parts of this region women form a third of the working population. Along the coast, one commonly finds women who have had three to seven husbands during their childbearing years. In other parts, especially the big ranches, women are still sold. This region leads the country in consumption of alcohol. It is the home of bestiality, and magic rites dominate in religion and in all areas of life.

The third zone in the mountains is characterized by the unmarried mother and by concubinage. Both men and women have strong opposition to being married in church. The woman feels she is in a stronger position if free to leave a man who ill-treats her, while the man feels that if he is not married to her the woman will make more effort to be pleasing and attractive.

Even in the first region, where Catholic marriage predominates, moral conditions are far from perfect. This is the part of the country in which prostitution is most highly institutionalized. Homosexuality is also prevalent, even in rural areas, as it also is in Bogotá. A possible factor is that in this region what amounts to a myth surrounds idealized womanhood, giving status but also remoteness to the woman.

In no area of the Church's life in Latin America does greater reticence exist than in that of finances, and it is difficult for the average North American, whether Catholic or not, to understand the elements involved. The first thing to note is the difference of background. The Catholic Church in the United States was historically charged with a single function, to administer the sacraments and perform strictly religious rites and ceremonies. Later there was added a task regarded as important by the members of the Church: the provision of educational facilities. Catholic schools have undoubtedly helped the general community, both culturally and financially, but the service they have supplied has not been essential to the community because they developed not to fill a social vacuum but to parallel and balance the existing public schools. Hospitals and other social services, though substantial, were always subsidiary. Few communities depended mainly on them. For the nation they were never more than marginal.

In Europe generally, the Church was the original creator and supplier of educational, health and social services for the entire community, a task formalized in Latin America by the Spanish monarchy's entrusting of these activities exclusively to the Church. From the start, it had a monopoly on civilizing and cultural activities, and the state pledged itself to give it the means needed to realize its social objectives. Great institutions, universities, hospitals, welfare organizations and churches resulted during the early period of expansion, all maintained by the grant of vast tracts of land. When the influence and activity of the Church dwindled in the eighteenth century, for the reasons already indicated, the ownership of these properties continued in the ecclesiastical corporations in which title had been vested. In the nineteenth century, anticlerical governments in many cases confiscated all Church property, sometimes without compensation, sometimes with arrangements to pay whatever annual amounts they decided would maintain such Church-directed activities as they considered socially desirable.

The resulting picture is very mixed. In some countries, an inventory would reveal an impressive accumulation of capital which further analysis would prove illusory. Lima, for example, has great numbers of magnificent churches dating back to the high point of culture in the sixteenth and seventeenth centuries, many of them on locations where land is now at a premium. Actually, these churches are a liability. The old city has become a business center with few residents, so that the cost of maintaining the buildings and staffing them is out of all proportion to the pastoral service they provide. Meanwhile, the rapidly growing new suburbs and even more rapidly growing slums lack churches and other parish facilities. I have mentioned Lima, where any visitor will immediately be struck by the magnificence and number of the churches, but the situation can be paralleled in most of the cities of Latin America. Often the churches are architectural monuments, and always they have emotional ties. The suggestion that some of them should be pulled down is met by cries of outrage, if not by counter-suggestions that the proposal is Communist-inspired.

Other properties held by the Church, originally intended to produce revenue or to house Church-directed social activities, have experienced the decline characteristic of the entire economy, and today frequently do no more than pay for themselves. These may consist of elaborate but utterly inefficient eighteenth-century buildings occupying great space in city locations that now have major value as building sites, or vast tracts of land still farmed under the hacienda system. As an illustration of the difference between actual and potential income in such cases, I may note that the Rector of San Marcos University recently said that 500,000 square feet of rental property owned by the university in Lima was producing annual income of under $75,000, when it should be producing $800,-000 at the going rate. San Marcos, founded under Church auspices in 1551, was nationalized in the last century, but its problem of under-productive endowments remains the same as that of properties still in Church ownership. Such holdings have been treasured for their prestige value, even when producing only nominal income, but today it is being recognized that the impression they create is an unfavorable one, and that both the Church and the national economy would benefit from disposing of them.

The end result is that in spite of, and perhaps to some extent because of, the presence of these nominal but unproductive assets, the average priest is miserably poor. Some own only a single cassock, without a suit to go under it. Ownership of an automobile or jeep is usually unthinkable, even if a parish extends fifty miles from end to end or has twenty thousand inhabitants. The priest usually has few sources of income beyond a small salary paid by the bishop from endowments or from state subsidies. Such sources of funds are dwindling, because the endowments normally consist of dying assets like those just described, and the tendency of the state is toward divorcing itself progressively from religion.

Indicative of the new attitudes within the Church was the announcement early in 1962 that the bishops of Chile had decided to sell farms and estates belonging to the country's various dioceses. The announcement came while an agrarian reform law was before Congress. The bishops said their step was intended as an example for all Chileans. It may be anticipated that similar action will be taken by other bishops in similar circumstances.

As in Europe, so in Latin America, the traditional supplement to state help was gifts from the wealthy, a source which has also declined with the secularization and drifting away from the Church of many in the upper classes. Besides, when the rich pay, they control, and today a belief on the part of the poor that the Church is allied to the rich creates an impassable barrier to the exercise of the apostolate. Dictators like Perón in Argentina and Trujillo in the Dominican Republic went to great lengths to buy the approval or at least the silence of the Church. Because of their arbitrary power, they were capable of creating complicated and compromising situations. The Church undoubtedly suffered through the indiscretions of some clergymen who allowed themselves to be used by the dictators, but on the whole, it has emerged very well from the principal recent experiences of this kind.

The normal United States approach to parish financing by small but regular contributions from all communicants is practically unknown in Latin America. Few countries in the world, if any, have so highly organized and developed a system of fund-raising as ours, and indeed the average Latin American Catholic finds our system, in which the pastor of a suburban parish operates a streamlined business with a budget of often a quarter million dollars a year, not only unattractive but positively disturbing.

It is nevertheless becoming recognized that from now on the parish will have to look mainly to the poor for its support, and greater effort is being devoted to developing among the members the concept of participation in a common effort which is the key to the success of the United States technique.

I even have come across an amusing effort at adaptation. In many Latin American countries, the lottery is the standard device for raising money for charity, and in a church in a remote part of Colombia, I was recently handed by the priest a slip of paper in return for the contribution I had dropped in the collection plate at Sunday Mass. On examining the slip, I found it was a numbered ticket entitling the holder to a chance on one tenth of the collection. A similar slip was given to each person who contributed one peso (12¢) or more.

In spite of the inducement, few people around me contributed more than a small part of a peso. The poverty is extreme, and the habit of giving is acquired slowly. I know a church in Lima where the thousand people who attend Sunday Mass contribute between them eight or nine dollars. A big city church in Rio collects five dollars from 7,500 Mass-goers. A country church near Santa Cruz, Bolivia, averages fifty cents. In a church in Manizales, Colombia, I heard the pastor report cash outlays of $250 during the previous month, and income from the Sunday collection of just under ten dollars.

In the United States, even among Catholics, the view is not infrequently prevalent that the priests themselves are largely to blame for the low level of Catholic practice in Latin America. The inadequacy of this explanation of an admitted fact will be evident from the foregoing. In addition, it must be understood that Latin American priests inevitably share the cultural characteristics and social attitudes of the society to which they belong. If life has long been characterized by a negative attitude toward work, a sense of being trapped within a system against which it would be useless to struggle, an easy-going identification of the actual with the inevitable, one must not be surprised to find these same values accepted among the clergy. All too often, moreover, the fewness of priests meant that the intellectual and cultural training of candidates had to be skimped, young men being placed in charge of parishes with little of the competence or specialized preparation the task required. What is extraordinary is that so many of them continued to maintain a small center of Catholic activity around the church building, even if they failed to move out into other areas of life in the far-flung parishes.

No little discussion has been devoted to the question of whether in such circumstances it is proper at all to describe Latin America as a Catholic region, a valid question in assessing both the propriety of Protestant mission activity and of certain types of Protestant missionary approach as well as the Catholic reaction to them. One can come up with very contradictory answers, according to the context of the question, the bias of the questioner, and the semantic vagaries of language.

On the one side, probably as many as 80 per cent of Latin Americans are baptized in the Catholic Church and regard themselves as Catholics. On this basis, one-third of the world's Catholics are located in Latin America. On the other hand, as Pope Pius XII said in 1955, Catholicism in this region reveals deficiencies which become more serious by the day. And Pope John XXIII, in November 1958, said to the Latin American Bishops' Council: "The tenacity, the sincerity and the vigor of the faith rooted in the peoples of Latin America is not always accompanied, as it should be, by a practice of that faith, whether in the life of the individual, in the family, or in society."

The situation was summed up in 1955 by the *Civiltà Cattolica*, a magazine published in Rome by the Italian Jesuits, as follows: "The practicing Catholics who in Latin America observe the fundamental laws and precepts of the Church come to between 15 and 30 per cent of the entire population, including young children." A pastoral letter of the bishops of Chile the previous year had said that only ten per cent of the Catholics of that country could be classed as practicing. A study by the Young Christian Workers in Paraguay two years later revealed that 80 per cent of young workers of Paraguay had made their First Communion, but that they had then given up all practice of their religion.

The extent and direction of Protestant penetration has to be related to these facts. The organized efforts at Protestant missionary work go back on a pilot scale to the last century, but it is only comparatively recently that they have assumed major proportions. Today they are massive, especially since the expansion of the Communist empire in Europe and Asia in the 1950's and restrictions on mission work in India and Indonesia have cut down other areas of mission activity.

In the early days, the Catholic reaction was a combination of outrage and incredulity, outrage at the idea of Christian missionaries purporting to bring Christianity to an area that had been Christian for centuries, disbelief that Latin Americans could ever be anything but Catholics because of their rapid acceptance of and age-long devotion to Catholicism. However, in the light of the inability of the Catholic Church to reach in any meaningful manner a vast number of Latin Americans, it is difficult to question the judgment or intentions of Protestant missionaries who seek to propagate in these areas the beliefs they must be presumed to hold in good faith. In the light of their success in many areas, it is no longer permissible to assume that Latin Americans possess some sort of mystic immunity to Protestantism.

The problem has, however, been embittered by the techniques of some of the missionaries, largely members of the fringe evangelical sects who have themselves abandoned most of the doctrines and the ecclesiastical structure held in common by Catholics and the major Protestant denominations. Their approach has frequently been in the form of a hostile and aggressive denunciation of the "decadent Catholic Church of Latin America," and it has produced reactions which though often deplorable are frequently understandable. The recognized Protestant bodies, on the contrary, have usually operated on a level of strict propriety.

It seems more necessary than ever, in the light of the present Holy Father's emphasis on Church unity, to stress this distinction and attempt to evaluate the positive elements, or at least the good faith and Christian inspiration of the Protestant mission movement. As far back as 1910, at a Protestant international mission conference at Edinburgh, Scotland, delegates from the United States declared their conviction that "millions and millions of Latin Americans find themselves to all intents and purposes deprived of the word of God and do not even know what the Gospel is." Action was nevertheless postponed after a serious discussion in the course of which European Protestant leaders, principally the German Lutherans, opposed the development of Protestant missions in Latin America on the ground that the region was not pagan but Catholic.

Three years later, however, a permanent Committee of Co-operation in Latin America was established at a conference in New York, and this was followed by regular congresses held in Latin American cities. The first of these, at Panama in 1916, developed interdenominational activities, seeking to divide up the territory among the different Protestant groups and achieve a maximum of cooperation in publishing and other fields. From this movement grew Protestant seminaries in Argentina, Brazil, Chile, Mexico, Puerto Rico, and Uruguay, and propaganda bureaus in Brazil, Cuba, Chile, Puerto Rico, and Uruguay. Gradually, missions to the Indians of Mexico, Peru and the Amazon basin were also begun.

Statistics confirm the increase in the Protestant effort. In 1903, only 3 per cent of Protestant missionaries were in the region. By 1937, the percentage had grown to 7 per cent. In 1959, one quarter of Protestant missionaries were at work here, and a special secretariat general for Latin America had come into being. Church membership had become substantial. Figures compiled by the Missionary Research Library in New York in 1957 list over six million Protestants for the Latin American mainland and the Caribbean islands, and claims as high as ten million are now being made. Perhaps more significant is the high proportion of nationals among the Protestant clergy. In spite of the rapid growth in the number of outside missionaries, the non-nationals represented only one-third of the total in 1957, permitting a spokesman to declare that Latin American Protestantism was no longer an imported product, but possessed a national community in each country, directed principally by South Americans, "a spiritual reality that has taken flesh in South America."

Protestant mission methods are varied. They stress direct preaching in meeting halls, in the open air, in hospitals, at home, even on river boats, and they devote much effort to the distribution of written materials, from tracts to books. The Bible naturally gets top emphasis, with a distribution of half a million copies as far back as 1915, an annual rate that had risen to six and a half million forty years later. Radio is likewise important, many transmitters being owned by a Protestant church or group of churches. Best known is the powerful Voice of the Andes in Quito, Ecuador, which transmits programs for twenty sects that can be heard easily as far south as Argentina and consequently blanket the entire continent.

Education has also proved a powerful means of penetration. Primary and secondary schools draw pupils by the quality of their instruction and by the special attraction which the English language today has in all countries. A continuing stress on the training of pastors and leaders is reflected in an increase in the number of seminaries to fifty, and of Bible schools to one hundred and fifty. Interdenominational seminaries for several churches or mission societies exist in Argentina, Brazil, Puerto Rico and Mexico.

One must, accordingly, recognize the fact of the presence of Protestantism in every country and city of Latin America. Everywhere one sees Protestant churches and meeting halls side by side with the Catholic churches. Many countries accord complete equality before the law to all religions. Even in those in which some degree of privilege is retained by the Catholic Church, the newcomers suffer in practice little or no disability.

Nor is their radius of activity confined to the cities. In Peru, for example, the largest single unit of Protestants is in the high Andes, near historic Lake Titicaca, where the Seventh-Day Adventists operate a network of one hundred and fifty elementary and two secondary schools among the Quechua Indians, as well as a small hospital, clinics, and training schools for religious teachers. Indians educated in these schools go from door to door to win converts, with the result that this sect has some 25,000 well-trained followers. The moral teaching they impart stresses the evil of drinking, gambling and blasphemy, giving the group an excellent reputation because of the exemplary lives lived by its members.

Initial Catholic reaction tended, perhaps understandably, to be emotional rather than logical. However, it gradually became obvious that polemics based on the theological arguments developed by the Counter-Reformation in the seventeenth century to stem the onrush of the Protestant Reformation had little relevance to the new conflict. And at least some Catholics came to recognize that one had no right to speak of formal heresy and bad faith in the case of the adherence to a Protestant group of one baptized a Catholic but lacking both intellectual formation in his religion and training in its practices and devotions.

Actually, the place where the phenomenon of Protestant penetration of a Latin American community has been most scientifically studied is New York, one of whose curious socio-religious developments has been the growth of the so-called store-front churches among the Puerto Ricans. Any observer could see an extraordinary fervor among their adherents. They spent long hours in services. They contributed freely from their small wages. They visited the sick in hospitals and worked feverishly to win others to membership. Their own explanations, however, seemed inadequate to explain their conversion, and in fact they are totally wide of the mark, although admittedly sincere. "I was very sinful," a man will say, interpreting the change in the simplified theological terms absorbed at the meeting hall. "I went with women, and I drank too much. Then the spirit came and changed my life."

The true motivation seems to be something quite different. Sociologists use the term *anomie* to describe the emotional state of those who lose their customary group relationships in the change from one culture to another, or from the countryside to the city. Unable to cope with the challenges of the new environment, they grow insecure and cease to experience a sense of purpose and pattern in life. Religion can help to bridge this chasm, but in the case in question religion had not been an active part of their former life, and it was not institutionalized for them in such a way as to provide forms enabling them to reestablish.

For such people the store-front church supplied a vital need. It created a sense of community, formed a brotherhood, provided an opportunity to give something to others—what the sociologists call the we-feeling, the dependency-feeling and the role-feeling. The theological content of these is frequently marginal, making it easy to train leaders and clergymen, and also minimizing the seriousness of the transfer of allegiance from Catholicism for those who might have some scruples of conscience.

It seems clear that similar factors have counted heavily in the growth of Protestantism in all Latin American countries. In the cities is found the phenomenon of the rapid building up of great masses of people transferred from a rural society without any preparation, and thrust into slum conditions which destroy any sense of dignity and self-respect they may have. For them, membership in a group which welcomes them and encourages self-expression provides the same emotional values as the Puerto Ricans find in the store-front church in New York. Even in rural areas Latin Americans of the lower classes find themselves in a similar condition of divorce from their surroundings and rejection by the society in which they live. This is particularly true of the Indians of the high plateaus of the Andes. Far from living the contented, idyllic lives which many of us conveniently ascribe to them, they suffer from a high incidence of emotional disturbance. Hundreds of years of dependence have given them a deep pessimism about their ability to regain control of their individual and group destinies. It is among these people that the Adventists have made the progress mentioned above, and among them the Communists have also made great inroads.

On the margin of the organized religious groups are to be found numbers of sects appealing to the ignorance and superstition of their followers. It is usually impossible to distinguish in them any coherent body of religious belief or practice. They thrive because of the material advantages they offer their members, or because they fulfill the kind of emotional function already described. They may have political overtones or engage in activities running counter to established social patterns. Various sects from the United States coming under the general heading of "revivalists" are found in this group. It also includes faith healers, who at times assemble great masses of followers.

These marginal sectarians are to blame for much of the ill-will against Protestant missionaries which exists in Catholic circles in Latin America. They blame the Catholic Church for the ignorance of the masses and their lack of religious practice, and their principal proselytizing weapon is apt to be a virulent denunciation of the priest as a parasite living on the poor and giving nothing back. Naturally, their approach does not sit well with the village priest, particularly where such an allegation may seem to have some basis in fact. In the Spanish tradition, the local administrator has always had wide discretion in the methods he uses to maintain public order, and the machinery of redress for the victim of his abuse of his powers has seldom been effective. One can, accordingly, see what happens if one or two outsiders—especially if they are foreigners—come into a village in which the priest has traditionally enjoyed prestige and a major voice in community affairs, and begins to denounce him openly as a limb of Satan and despoiler of the people. It may not be defensible, but it certainly is not surprising, if in such circumstances the people take the law into their own hands and run the offenders out of town. Quite frequently, the priest will not even have to drop a hint. The mayor and he will merely have to look the other way.

At times local political divisions compound the problem, as happened particularly in Colombia during the 1950's. As has been earlier noted, savage and often quite irrational violence rent that country from 1948 onward, resulting in several hundred thousand killings, more than the number killed in battle in any war ever fought in the hemisphere, including our own Civil War. The strife in many areas assumed the form of a clash between Conservatives, priding themselves on their loyalty to the Church, and traditionally anticlerical Liberals. Protestant mission activity became associated in the popular mind with the Liberal side, and many of the much publicized attacks on Protestant missions and personnel were simply aspects of the broader conflict, although they were interpreted in the United States as a persecution of religion.

Another aspect of the religious situation which has probably been far more publicized than the realities warrant is the survival of pagan rites, often set in a framework of Christian ceremonies. The best known are the voodooism of Haiti and the related *candomblé* of Bahia state and other parts of Brazil, both tracing back to Africa. Also widespread in Brazil, and practiced to a lesser extent in Argentina and other countries, is the type of spiritism or spiritualism which had a vogue in the United States and Britain more than half a century ago. Elsewhere, one finds many survivals of pre-discovery religious practices among the Indians of Guatemala, Bolivia, Peru and Ecuador. What the African and Indian survivals principally demonstrate is how much still remains to be done in order to complete the work of conversion by the development of a culture solidly based on Catholic practices.

9

+ – + – *Leadership from Within*

W<small>HAT</small> <small>STRENGTHS</small> <small>AND</small> <small>SUCCESSES</small>
balance the weaknesses and problems of the Church in Latin Amer-
ica outlined in the last chapter? Bishop Rafael Larraín of Chile, a
vice-president of the Latin American Bishops' Council and one of
the most outspoken exponents of the need for social reform, recently singled out four basic favorable elements. "I am optimistic
about the future," he told me, "because of the profound faith in
the soul of the people, their deep sense of charity and anxiety to
help one another, particularly evident among the very poor, their
deep and solid devotion to the Blessed Virgin, and the extraordinary development of Catholic Action and the lay apostolate in the
past twenty-five years."

The organization which has most caught the imagination of Latin Americans and seems best to respond to their need is the Young Christian Workers. They have taken root and grown rapidly in most countries. I have seen them in action from Cuba to Chile, and everywhere they show a remarkable enthusiasm and a great dedication. They concentrate on the formation of leaders who combine deep knowledge of their faith with thorough training in social questions, especially as related to their environment. The primary function of these specialists is less to develop activities of the group itself than to participate in community projects, seeking to impress on them a Christian stamp. Many of the leaders of Christian trades unions and of the political parties of Christian inspiration have graduated from the Young Christian Workers. Their influence has made itself felt even in areas of deficient culture, such as the plantations of Guatemala and the slums of Santiago and Buenos Aires. It should be noted, however, that excellent as are these active workers, their numbers are still so small as usually to permit only pilot projects. The society in general has hardly begun to feel their impact.

An associated organization, the Young Christian Students Movement, is exercising a similar influence in the universities, traditionally dominated by left-wing and anticlerical elements. Here, too, the purpose is less to create new organizations than to form groups of activists who will participate in existing student movements, presenting positive policies of social progress in an area long preempted by subversives and radicals.

The university in Latin America can challenge the system of land tenure for the distinction of being the institution most out of tune with the region's needs. First of all, there is the inadequacy of facilities for the intellectual and professional needs of an emerging society. With a bigger population than the United States, Latin America has only one tenth the number of university students.

While we spend on the average well over a thousand dollars a year on each student, they spend two hundred dollars. In other words, their total expenditure on university education is about 2 per cent of ours.

An inevitable result is an extreme inadequacy of physical facilities, especially in medicine and the sciences, and starvation wages for professors. Few faculty members work full time. In Peru, only eleven per cent of the country's 1,280 professors were full time during 1959–61. The others work for prestige rather than money, with consequent lack of control over their attendance, the content of their teaching or their pedagogical methods. There is little supervision of the academic standards of the students, and even less effort to direct them into socially desirable programs. Law schools are swollen far beyond community needs, while teachers, doctors and engineers are lacking. Students who do not attend class or pass examinations are often retained for years, sources of disturbance and demoralization for their companions as well as wasters of inadequate facilities.

All these defects are associated with a time lag in the definition of the function of the university in the community. In its origin, the university in Latin America was a place of privilege for members of the upper class. As society became more complicated and required more professionals, university intake was expanded to include youths drawn from the upper middle class and form them in the mentality required to function in a strict class society as fringe members of the upper class. In this century, with the rapid creation of a middle class seeking to assert itself and reject the tutelage of the upper class, the university changed its function radically, becoming the center and means of expression of middle-class discontent and frustrations.

Most European countries went through a similar experience of university domination by radical political movements during the growth of the middle classes, but the European universities recovered rapidly, thanks in part to their more firmly rooted academic traditions, in part to the speed with which the middle class triumphed. Latin American universities are suffering from the slow evolution of the middle class to the extreme that politics has replaced learning as their specific function. This is true to the amazing extent that many of the big national universities have introduced institutional reforms to increase student control of administration and give the students a voice in national affairs similar to that of the Church and the army. It should, however, be added that the creation of a political conscience among university students is not entirely negative. The idealism of the young at times becomes the greatest challenge to the stagnation of political life, bringing public opinion to bear on unresolved national problems. The Latin American student's dedication to his ideals contrasts favorably with the hedonistic and anti-social concerns of many United States college students, particularly in Catholic colleges cut off from the main stream of community preoccupations.

Since World War II, the Communists have made great efforts to benefit from these conditions, concerning themselves with student reform movements, political attitudes such as anti-colonialism and anti-imperialism, national social programs, and the value standards of society. Both Russia and China have brought Latin American students in substantial numbers to visit their respective countries. China has not attempted to offer them specialized training, but simply to show them the progress being made by the new regime. Russia, however, in addition to propaganda, has created or adapted courses designed to attract Latin Americans.

The United States has also shown concern. The Rockefeller Foundation, for example, has made major contributions, especially to the development of technical facilities in agriculture and medicine. Other foundations which have shown substantial interest in-

clude the Kellogg, the Ford and the Carnegie. Various United
States universities, usually working with outside funds, have undertaken programs in cooperation with Latin American universities. A
1960 report estimated a total of sixty programs for which thirty
United States universities and colleges were responsible. The total
impact, nevertheless, is still only marginal. Aid on the scale envisaged in the Alliance for Progress is still needed if the Latin American university is to serve the needs of its society by turning out
the educated professionals and skilled technicians needed right
now.

Some 80 per cent of all universities in Latin America are official
or national. Most of the others are Catholic, mostly small, housed
in antiquated and run-down buildings, and suffering from even a
more acute shortage of funds than the state-subsidized universities.
Even so, their potential contribution to the development of Latin
America cannot be overestimated. They have fortunately escaped
the "reform" movement which has substituted politics for learning in many of the national universities; in them the relationship
of faculty to students and the students' concept of their duties and
purposes are far closer to our ideas. They would consequently respond much more rapidly to an infusion of professional assistance
from the United States. The only such assistance of which I am
aware was that given by Villanova University in the creation and
development of Villanueva University in Havana, and unfortunately that magnificent chapter in the life of the Church in
Latin America was prematurely interrupted by the Communist
take-over of Cuba and the seizure of the university. A combined
effort by the Catholic universities of this country, similar to the
recent initiative of the Catholic Press Association of the United
States taken in behalf of its Latin American colleagues, would
undoubtedly pay big dividends. The press program, begun in 1959,

produced an exchange of information and analysis of problems in 1960, followed by a series of seminars in several Latin American countries in 1961, in which United States newsmen discussed the techniques of their trade with their Latin American colleagues of the Catholic press. Programs now being developed look to further training, exchange of newsmen, and modernization of plants. This approach is equally appropriate to the university field, both for academic matters and for such allied programs as university presses and publishing, highly developed here and sorely needed there.

Another area in which the Church has made little more than marginal impact is organized labor. The development of Christian trades unions has been difficult. The reason has been in part the absence of the basic conditions required for any labor organization, education of the workers, a sense of community of interest among the workers, a status in society enabling the worker through the union to meet his employer on a level of approximate equality, or at least to exercise substantial economic power. The status of the worker involves political, social and economic elements. He needs certain legal protections and guarantees for his organizations. He needs a public attitude and outlook sympathetic to his claims. He needs a balance between the labor requirements and the labor force in the community.

In all these respects, labor is at a grave disadvantage in Latin America. Because of control of legislatures and administrations by elements unsympathetic to labor, legislation has been slow in developing, limited in scope, and ineffectively applied. The gap between worker and employer has been so wide as to make any effort of the former to assert his rights seem an outrageous violation of the established order. The endemic surplus of labor has made it ordinarily impossible to maintain a united front in a showdown. Employers have been able to break strikes and crush unions by drawing replacements from the bottomless pit of the destitute unemployed, to whom a job offer necessarily outweighed any theoretic consideration of fraternal solidarity.

Under such conditions, the type of union we know in the United States can scarcely thrive. In Latin America unions spring up and wither away in response to local conditions. They function as personal groupings around a strong man who can protect his followers rather than as impersonal expressions of ideological policy. They look to politics rather than to collective bargaining to win concessions.

The Christian trades union movement has suffered from additional handicaps. Up to a quarter century ago, as already indicated, the division of forces in Latin America followed the evolution which had occurred earlier in Europe, with the party of progress strongly anticlerical and committed to socialist, anarchist, communist and other extreme left-wing theories. The original trades union movement began under these influences. For the basic reasons explained above, it never developed into a mass movement with a solid and coherent policy. Instead, it has floundered about in the wake of political parties, searching for opportunistic advantages, and subordinating the real interests of the workers in general to the immediate benefit of small privileged groups who in special circumstances were able to create artificial islands of prosperity for themselves alongside the misery of their comrades.

Always opportunists, many of these during and immediately after World War II ranged themselves openly in the Communist camp as affiliates of the Communist-organized and dominated World Federation of Trades Unions. However, as the Cold War progressed, they recognized that they would do better to switch sides to the International Confederation of Free Trades Unions, to which the main body of United States organized labor, AFL-CIO, is affiliated, and which enjoys great influence and access to im-

portant funds because of the favor with which it is looked upon by
the United States government and United States labor. Since
United States government and labor are officially committed to
this faction, they must of necessity ignore and deny their help to,
if not actively oppose, the competing movement affiliated to the
International Federation of Christian Trades Unions.

A definite factor in the forming of United States public opinion on this subject has been a mistaken projection into Latin
America of conditions in this country. The trades union movement
in the United States functions on a basis which is formally neutral
in relation to organized religions, but which reflects the viewpoints and interests of the religious groups which constitute the
great bulk of union members. There never evolved here any movement based on denominational affiliation, and no body of responsible opinion in any of the denominations ever favored such a development. All representative leaders of our labor movement,
including the Catholics who played a major part in the creation of
labor organizations and an equally decisive part in preventing their
perversion to left-wing political ends in the 1930's, have always regarded the religious neutrality of the unions as one of their pillars
of strength.

The error, however, has been to accept the argument that the
self-styled free trades unions of Latin America reflect the favorable
and positive attitudes toward religion of the United States movement, because they are affiliated to the same International, and
because both are constitutionally neutral in religious matters.
These unions are "neutral" in the European and not in the American sense, neutral *against* and not neutral *for*. If today, for opportunistic reasons, they reject Marxism, they nevertheless adhere
to the tradition of the class war, and many of them not only call
themselves socialist but preach a version of socialism and class
hatred which is far to the left of Marxism, more Trotskyite than

Fabian. There is no common ground between them and what we call the American way of life, and the current alliance rests on deception on one side and a semantic misunderstanding compounded by ignorance on the other.

The unions affiliated to the Christian federation are in fact much closer to our concept of trades unionism. In spite of the inclusion of the word *Christian* in their title, they are not denominational unions. In parts of Asia, for example, they include large numbers of Buddhists and other non-Christians among their members. What they stand for is rather the concept of social organization and cooperation of the classes proclaimed in the papal encyclicals, principles stemming from the Judaeo-Christian tradition and accepted alike by Catholics, Protestants and Jews. If the United States must make a choice in Latin America, the much more logical one is this.

Many however feel, and I found this viewpoint strongly expressed by some Young Christian Worker leaders, that the split between the free and Christian unions cannot be ended by a fight to the finish between the two movements. While each is weak, both are strong enough to hang on indefinitely, to the continuing loss of the workers for whose benefit they exist, and to the advantage of the Communist unions which thrive on their disunion. What these people believe is that a basis for broad understanding, if not a total merger, must be reached by developing a formula similar to the one that has worked so well in the United States. This would cut the unions completely away from the Socialist and Christian Democratic political movements, leaving as their sole function the protection of the economic interests of the workers, within a framework that would be formally neutral in religious matters but basically Christian. Substantial progress has been made in hammering out such a formula in Europe, but Latin America's traditional time lag in the area of ideas operates to delay for emotional reasons a development the logic of which is already apparent.

The official attitude of the Young Christian Workers towards labor movements in Latin America was formulated at a meeting of the international executive committee in Havana in 1959. YCW, it said, is an educational movement which cannot be identified with or considered tied to any labor organization. It fights for freedom of labor and the expansion of free and democratic trades unions in all countries. While leaving its branches in each country free to fix their relationship with unions operating in that country, it recognizes that many of its members in fact belong to trades unions affiliated with the Christian International, and many to unions affiliated with the Free International. In consequence, it urges increased cooperation between the two bodies to promote labor solidarity and progress.

Other aspects of the awakened interest of Latin America's Catholics in social problems have been worked out in recent years at three rural life conferences. The inspiration for these reunions, held in Colombia, Panama, and Chile, came largely from the National Catholic Rural Life Conference of the United States. The meetings focused attention on rural needs, defined concrete action programs for the leaders of society called upon to translate principles into institutions, and helped to form these leaders as Christian social actionists.

The new look is also being developed in the formal statements of bishops. "A serious sin and the greatest danger of our times" were the words used in a collective pastoral of the Latin American Bishops' Council, after its 1960 meeting at Fomeque, Colombia, to describe the underdevelopment and hunger suffered by two-thirds of Latin Americans. Catholics, they added, must dedicate themselves to ending the huge economic and social differences which divide the people.

Many bishops have stressed, and continue to stress, the obligation to pay just wages, the need to extend social legislation to all who need its benefits, and the national obligation to raise the living standards of the poorest citizens. In this connection, one may point to three pastorals of the late Cardinal Caro of Chile, a man with a profound social sense, a collective pastoral of the bishops of Peru in 1959, a pastoral of the Archbishop of Lima in 1960, the impassioned declaration of the Archbishop of Guatemala in 1958 that "the measure of divine justice cannot continue to bear this iniquitous exploitation," a 1960 pastoral of the bishops of Colombia backing a land reform project then bogged down in that country's Congress, a declaration of Bishop Larraín of Talca, Chile, in 1961, that absolutely nothing was so urgent as an improvement in the rural population's standard of living, an improvement which must include a more equitable distribution of the land.

Probably the best known work under Church auspices in Latin America today is Colombia's Rural Cultural Action, headed by Monsignor Joaquin Salcedo, developer of techniques for teaching literacy by radio which are today being imitated in many countries. Assigned as pastor to the remote mountain village of Sutatenza in the Andes in the mid-forties, Father Salcedo soon learned the facts of rural life. Seventy per cent of his 7,000 parishioners were illiterate. Fewer than two hundred of them lived in the village clustered around the church, the rest being scattered over sixty square miles of untracked mountainside, experiencing entirely different agricultural and climatic conditions according to their location on slopes which produced a change of more than six thousand feet in altitude between the highest and lowest points in the parish. They lived in windowless shacks, which he quickly dubbed "antihygienic forts." Abuse of alcohol, their only escape from intolerable reality, was widespread.

Father Salcedo decided that it was a waste of time simply to denounce the taverns. He had to replace them. And he decided to draw to his side a modern miracle hitherto unknown in Sutatenza. He arranged a film showing in the main square one evening in August 1947. The results were so overwhelming that he easily organized a labor force to build a movie house. Long a radio ham, he decided to use a small transmitter to help round up his workers, and almost before he realized, Radio Sutatenza was born.

Responding to the initiative of their priest, the parishioners contributed in work, money and kind. One appeal brought in 800 chickens, sold in the Bogotá market. A 250-watt transmitter was bought for two thousand dollars from United States war surplus stocks, and Father Salcedo began his literacy lessons to fifteen radio schools on Saturday afternoons.

The radio school is the home of a villager who can read and write. He is in charge of the session, which has now developed from its original crude form, thanks to the technical help of UNESCO and other educational organizations, into a scientific operation. Each school receives simple teaching aids, a blackboard, chalk, notebooks, texts, even an alarm clock to announce the start of transmission. The simply constructed radio sets are bought by individuals or cooperatively.

Educational broadcasts from six transmitters located at Bogotá, Sutatenza and Balencito have expanded to ten hours daily and reach 140,000 students of all ages in twelve of Colombia's sixteen departments. Nearly 40,000 of the special radio receivers have been distributed. Today, the work is directed and the programs prepared in an imposing center in Bogotá. But transmissions still orginate at Sutatenza, where the modern, powerful radio installations now include a 50-kilowatt transmitter, one of five.

To teach reading and writing to someone living in a remote rural area is, however, of little benefit, unless he can constantly be fed reading materials useful to him and geared to his cultural level and background. As I mentioned earlier, this is one of the great roadblocks to literacy in Latin America. Much of Mexico's vast effort among its Indians has been wasted because of the lack of follow-through with reading materials.

In this respect, also, Monsignor Salcedo has been an innovator. In addition to a major operation as a publisher of pamphlets and leaflets, he began a few years ago a weekly newspaper designed and produced exclusively for his newly literate peasants, and created to a major extent each week out of the news and comments which they supply to the editors about the activities of the more than two thousand schools with 215,000 registered students. This is a unique newspaper, modernly and attractively produced, now distributing 120,000 copies a week in 978 towns and villages of Colombia. No other weekly newspaper sells as many copies.

Literacy, however, is mainly a tool to be used in order to achieve better living. The self-reliance generated by Cultural Rural Action in the peasant who has learned to read and write is channeled into other self-help activities by its "Crossroads" movement. About a thousand Crossroads committees, consisting of leaders of the mountain hamlets, have been created. With help from the government's Community Action division, they built 5,000 homes in 1960 alone, improved 9,000 others, laid 2,300 community water systems, built 8,000 outhouses, smoothed out 1,350 playing fields, and organized 4,000 amateur theater groups.

Many of those active in this movement had been trained in the center known as the Rural Institutes of Sutatenza which has been operating since 1954. Here, rural young people in their upper teens are given six-month courses on how to improve the moral and material conditions of life in their villages. The centers, one for boys and one for girls, have trained 3,500 village leaders in eight years.

Other activities include leaflets, phonograph records and lending libraries, all organized on what is a principle of the movement, namely, to make available cultural elements to rural people but not to give them as gifts. "We are against paternalism," Monsignor Salcedo says. "What we are trying to do is to make the rural people see their problems, analyze them, and take steps to solve them."

Less known but probably not less important than the radio schools in Colombia are the more recently established Institutes of Rural Education in Chile. Also founded by a priest, their aim is to train village leaders in intensive courses held at centers, each of which consists of a demonstration farm, classroom, dormitories and other facilities for fifty resident students. The first center opened in 1955 had grown to twelve by 1961, with seventeen more scheduled for 1962 and 1963. The centers give a basic three-month course, allowing graduation of four classes yearly. The pace is gruelling, with over 400 hours of classes and many more hours of fieldwork and demonstrations. Top students are picked for advanced courses and are then sent as paid community leaders to form village centers.

Of 3,500 graduates of the centers at the end of six years of operation, several hundred were full-time community leaders, while the others were working on their parents' farms or were married and farming for themselves. The village leader program had started experimentally, even before the first center was functioning, with a dozen young people qualified more by enthusiasm than training. Experience refined the techniques. Village leaders meet each month for an orientation session at the center nearest their work, spend a month each year in refresher classes. Their primary job is as catalysts. They encourage the villagers to define their needs, then plan ways to realize them. Specifically, they promote better home conditions, sanitary and health practices, vegetable gardens, carpentry shops, grafting of fruit trees, disinfecting outhouses, vaccinating animals, organizing sports and amusements. Often they become emergency infirmarians, giving injections or bringing the gravely ill to hospital.

The primary aim of the training is to develop internal leadership in the villages, so that neither economic level nor previous education determines the choice of candidates. Tuition, board and lodging at the centers are free, and classes are organized at three levels of comprehension: for those learning to read and write, for those with grade schooling, and for those with some high school. As in most countries, so in Chile education has been city-centered, most of the teachers being city folk, and even those born in the country being city oriented by their training. To counter this, the centers organize vacation courses for rural school teachers similar to those they give their own students, and they distribute teaching aids to them throughout the year to help them give their students a professional preparation for rural living, and a love and knowledge of the soil.

The Institutes publish a monthly magazine geared to the needs and interests of the small farmer and his wife. Started in 1955, it had attained a circulation of 10,000 by 1962, impressive for a farm magazine in Chile. Educational radio programs, some intended for school use and others for home listening by farm families, began soon after the magazine. By 1959, there were six transmissions weekly, and the number was doubled by adding an advanced course in 1960. Six stations in 1958 grew to twenty in 1959 and forty-four in 1962. Eleven hundred schools were including the programs in the curriculum, most of them using radios supplied at cost by the Institutes. Chile with seven and a half million people is nearly 3,000 miles long, more than the distance from New York to Los Angeles, and only 110 to 222 miles wide. Institutes are developing family programs to supplement those for schools.

That and other advances will be greatly speeded by an agreement, signed in November 1961, with the United States Association for International Development, formerly Point Four, under which the Institutes were given a grant of $575,000 for their work.

The Institutes are legally organized as a voluntary, non-profit, non-denominational educational organization. They work in close cooperation with and get help from Chile's ministries of education, agriculture and health. Under Chilean law, any recognized institution giving secondary or technical education is subsidized in proportion to the number of students. This makes the centers practically self-sustaining and permits indefinite expansion, subject only to obtaining capital funds to build and equip them. The grant from the United States will be devoted to building and equipment, making possible a major expansion of the work.

UNESCO has recognized the Institutes as an official project for its aid. They function as the rural executive organ of Catholic Charities of Chile (Caritas), handling distribution of powdered milk for school children and other U. S. surplus foods supplied by Catholic Relief Services-NCWC. Other organizations from whom they receive help, or with which they cooperate, include the Argentine Rural Society, the Ken Davis Foundation, the Henry Lee and Grace Doherty Charitable Foundation, Braden Copper, Care, Misereor, and the Peace Corps.

The influence of the Institutes has already spread beyond the national frontiers. Twenty young Bolivians had been trained in the centers by the end of 1961, forty young Argentines, others from Peru, Ecuador, Brazil and Uruguay. Candidates in all cases were selected by their fellow villagers in cooperation with their pastor, and frequently with the active intervention of the bishop. All these countries are developing their own programs within the broad social development encouraged and inspired by the Church authorities.

"We already see enormous results," the head of the Institutes told me in 1961, when I inspected several of the centers. "Before, there were few cottage vegetable gardens. Now there are thousands. Before, few homes were concerned about latrines, clean

water, hygienic preparation of food. Now, young people want to
stay on the land. They are introducing better growing techniques.
Internal leadership is developing. Life is jollier. Fiestas have less
drunkenness and more fun. The people are asking us to start cooperatives, to advise them on credit for cottage industries, tools and
fertilizers. The young men want to farm for themselves."

Yet another success story illustrating the variety of forms in
which the new spirit of the Church in Latin America is expressing
itself, is that of the parish of Fomeque, a rural community of
14,000 inhabitants about thirty miles from Bogotá, Colombia.
This story goes back a little farther, to 1936, when a Father
Gutiérrez was named pastor of a rural parish typical in all respects,
in its low level of literacy, its poor housing and living conditions,
the indifferent practice of religion.

Father Gutiérrez decided that Fomeque had the resources, material and human, to rejuvenate itself, and he formed a socio-religious organization, a kind of general council of the rural community of Fomeque to plan and execute an operation envisaged on
three levels—economic, cultural and religious.

The economic plan began with programs on instruction and
joint action to improve housing, farming practices, care of domestic animals, and to establish home industries. As the project
progressed, credit and banking facilities were provided, electricity
was introduced, water reservoirs and aqueducts constructed, and
farm roads opened to all parts of the community.

The cultural programs stressed folk singing and dancing, gym-
nastics, sports. New perspectives and orientations were given to the
local fiestas. Health and hygienic practices were inculcated at the
individual, family and community levels. Homemaking and allied
activities were taught in a practical way by creating model farms
in various places where the neighbors could come and see in operation the techniques recommended for their imitation.

The religious side began with instructions based on the programs of the Congregation of Christian Doctrine. Lay catechists were given a solid foundation, and they in turn organized and taught classes for adults, for teen-agers, and for children. In addition to such standard religious practices as the Mass, confession, the family rosary, community singing in church, monthly retreats are held for each of several parish groups separately.

Twenty years after Father Gutiérrez had begun this series of programs, a United Nations official described Fomeque as a unique community. Public order was perfect, he said, and there had been only two crimes committed since the creation of the community council, one of them a crime of passion. Drunkenness had disappeared. The community had thirty-six primary schools, two schools for training rural teachers, two sections of a high school. The trained players engaged actively in sports programs numbered nine hundred. Farmers were well instructed in their work, and the community organization gave them the technical help they needed. A hospital had been opened and dwellings were being built and modernized according to a well-thought-out plan. "And above all," he concluded, "there is a constant intensification of Christian life, with the Gospel as the means, the beginning and the end."

El Salvador in Central America boasts another notable effort to meet religious needs with scant resources. It was begun in 1950 by the bishop of San Vicente, a diocese with 321,000 Catholics and only fifteen diocesan and seventeen religious priests, that is to say, more than ten thousand Catholics per priest.

The two big problems of the rural population are concubinage and drunkenness. Poverty, ignorance and sickness are caused or aggravated by constant consumption of an extremely potent alcoholic drink produced by fermenting rice or corn mixed with various fruit juices. Every man constantly carries a machete, and weekends and fiestas are commonly marked by bloody clashes.

The bishop's program began with the creation of an organization, to which he gave the name of Knights of Christ the King. Its purpose was to band the farmers together to enable them to take a more active part in the life of the Church and of the nation. The base unit is a cell of ten men, who picked their leaders, and these in turn form groups of ten leaders, and so on upwards. All the Knights meet monthly in their parishes, and the entire organization, now numbering twenty thousand, assembles once a year in the city of San Vicente.

The program of activities is similar to that already described for Fomeque in Colombia, but on an even bigger scale. They have, for example, planned and built many roads to give access to remote parts of the diocese, thereby also facilitating commercial transactions. Their help to agriculture has been remarkable. They have brought extension agents to the area to teach the farmer new techniques. They show educational films, and their monthly bulletin devotes a page to agriculture. They have made great strides in combating alcoholism, a success reflected in a notable reduction in major crimes.

In many villages they have opened schools to teach the rudiments of grammar and arithmetic. They have set up cooperatives, savings banks and credit unions. They provide urgently needed medicine, and they loan small sums to buy seeds. If a member falls sick, his companions tend and reap his crops, and if any of them loses his home for whatever reason, they build him a new one. The courts have entrusted to them the care of prisoners released on probation. For such a short time, the results are already truly impressive.

Elsewhere, unusual approaches to the problem of developing a parish life among people long out of touch with their priests are being tested. The parish of All Saints in Buenos Aires provides an interesting example. Its 20,000 inhabitants consist of civil servants and other middle-class elements, as well as working-class people, including those in a very poor section appropriately named the Black Cave. Here four priests have been working since 1951, and their card index now has records on nearly half of the parish's four thousand families. Of these, only a tiny nucleus, some fifty families, live a fully Christian life, while a further five hundred practice their religion fairly faithfully and attend Sunday Mass.

This approach to parish renewal is the more important because few problems are more urgent than to rebuild family life. In some countries, illegitimacy runs as high as 50 to 80 per cent, and living conditions in both rural and urban slums are such that children, while physically part of society, are not integrated into it either emotionally or culturally. The father declines his role as head of family, even when he lives in faithful concubinage and comes home to hand over his wages and to sleep. He spends whatever hours he can in the more congenial surroundings of the rum shop or the street-corner crap game. The mother's function is narrowed to the elemental emotions of the animal. She will fight and struggle to keep her children alive, but she loses concern for their intellectual or spiritual well-being. Love dies inside her. She does what she does without knowing or caring why she does it.

Starting from the premise that the Christian community should be built on the basis of the existing human community, the pastoral action at All Saints is developed in three concentric circles: the first formed by the priests and their active lay helpers, the second by the 500 practicing families, and the third by the entire community of 20,000 baptized but nominal Christians. The aim is to incorporate this mass in a single big community.

One approach is at the social level. Teams of helpers make contact with families or individuals who have human problems of illness, unemployment or lack of living quarters. They organize country vacations for the children, playgrounds, teams to donate blood, drawing the people by the practice of Christian charity in the direction of Christian hope and faith.

Another approach is at the religious level. Catholic Actionists visit homes to ask the family to receive the statue of the Blessed Virgin for a few days. In this way, the statue is transferred from house to house from Easter to December 8 each year. The visit of the Blessed Virgin provides the priest with a magnificent opportunity to get to know the family and neighbors. He blesses the house, says the rosary, speaks for twenty minutes on a doctrinal subject, and gives a copy of the Gospels to the head of the house.

Other Catholic Action teams prepare children for First Communion, taking advantage of the occasion not only to lay a foundation of Christian knowledge by means of a serious catechism course, but to develop attitudes in the family that will make more likely a continuance of Catholic practice after First Communion. For example, the mother must have two meetings with the pastor during the preparation period, and in addition, a priest must visit each home. After the ceremony, other teams follow up to encourage the children to celebrate the five big liturgical feasts of the years. Old traditions are, nevertheless, hard to break, and the percentage of those who persevere in religious practice after First Communion is still very low, the family attitude proving much more important than the level of religious instruction.

The priests, naturally, supervise all these activities, but they have also their own program of work. Five to six hundred visits are paid to the sick each year. When anyone dies, a priest visits the home, prays for the deceased, and uses the opportunity to explain the deep meaning of life and death. He offers to come back to lead the funeral procession to the church before burial, thus seizing an opportunity to speak to many people who would not otherwise cross his path. At each of the annual one hundred baptisms, he explains to a family the meaning of this sacrament. Before their marriage engaged couples are briefed on the duties they are assuming. District missions are preached all year round in private homes to small groups of neighbors, each mission lasting five days. So effective have they proved, that it is easy to recognize the sectors in which they have been held.

Other parishes have felt the radiation of the All Saints experiment, and already many pastors are adopting elements which seem to fit conditions in their own parishes, thereby multiplying the impact of a promising initiative.

For all the encouraging new life stirring within the Church in Latin America, it will have to lean heavily for long to come on foreign missionaries to supplement the work of native-born priests. Traditionally, Spain has been the primary source of outside help, performing a service that may in many respects be compared to that of Ireland for the Church in the United States in the nineteenth and early twentieth centuries.

The predominance of the Irish was not without its inconveniences in the United States, and the heavy dependence of the Church in Latin America on Spain has also produced its quota of problems. One bad aspect emerged dramatically in Cuba. When Castro wanted to blacken the Church, he was able to refer disparagingly to the priests from Spain as Fascists and lackeys of Franco. Although the blanket insult was certainly undeserved, it was precisely the kind of half-truth which United States public opinion is conditioned to swallow, and prevented the situation from being judged on its merits as a clear case of persecution of religion. It was, of course, a fact that about 400 of the 700 priests in Cuba were Spaniards, and some of them had not hidden their personal sympathy for the Franco regime in their homeland. If they had been Swiss or Belgian or Irish, it would have been less easy for the regime first to besmirch and later expel them.

Complete statistics of foreign missionaries in Latin America do
not exist. Many foreign-born priests and sisters have been natural-
ized, neither thinking of themselves nor being regarded as foreigners. Figures collected in 1960 in Colombia, a country which in
many respects is midway in development among Latin American
countries, show that 790 out of a total of 4,188 priests were foreign
born. Nearly half of the 123 foreign diocesan priests, and 62 per
cent of the 667 foreign religious priests were from Spain, with a
further 16 per cent from Italy and smaller percentages from Germany, France, Belgium, Holland, Switzerland, Canada, Venezuela, Ecuador and Mexico.

To coordinate and encourage mission work in Spain, an organization named Spanish-American Work of Priestly Cooperation was
set up in 1948, and by 1960 it had sent 350 priests to Latin America. Seminaries for this work function in Madrid, Saragossa and
Salamanca. The organization also encourages lay helpers to volunteer as teachers and catechists. Also from Spain are the members
of the Teresian Institution, a secular institute of women founded
in 1917, with a membership now exceeding two thousand. In
Latin America, where it has 33 houses, its members teach in universities, operate university residences, teacher training colleges,
secondary and primary schools, and various activities for intellectual and professional women.

A European College for Latin America was founded at Louvain
in 1954, and by the end of 1959 it had sent fifty priests to nine
countries, while 75 students, most of them from Belgium, were
studying at Louvain, in preparation for this work. In all, more than
250 mission priests from Belgium and more than a thousand from
Holland are in Latin America. Switzerland has lent a team of
priests to Colombia. German Fathers of the Divine Word are in
Argentina, Irish Columban Fathers in Peru, Italian Franciscans in
Central America. In mid-1962 the French bishops, at the request of

the Pope, set up a committee to organize the training of French diocesan priests for Latin America.

Both Canada and the United States are today deeply committed. A Bishops' Committee for Cooperation with Latin America coordinates the work of a thousand missionaries from Canada. The contribution from the United States is more than twice as big. Over two thousand priests, brothers and sisters, representing better than a third of the entire United States foreign mission personnel, are in Latin America.

The attitude of the Church in Latin America to missionaries coming from Europe has been summed up very well by Bishop José Dammert Bellido, of Peru. Having noted with appreciation the efforts of the hierarchies of different countries to encourage their priests to volunteer in substantial numbers, as urged by the Holy See, he warns the newcomers against dangerous misunderstandings. Latin America is not mission territory in the same sense as Africa, he points out. To misunderstand that is to fall into the same error as the Protestants who come to christianize a people Catholic for centuries. He continues: "We urgently need the help of both priests and lay people, since we are a new continent calling for the experience of other peoples at many levels, as priests, teachers, technicians, etc. But this help must be suited to our situation. Obviously, the idea must be got rid of that the object in coming is to make money. An unpleasant and indeed shameful memory lingers of certain cases in which the purpose of the trip was 'to come to America' (that is, to strike it rich), and those who came with such an attitude were truly wolves in sheep's clothing. . . . They caused their bishops a lot of trouble."

Recalling that Pius XII in his encyclical on the missions had stressed that the missionary must think of his new home as a second fatherland and love it as such, seeking neither earthly advantage nor the interest of his native land or of the mission institute to which he belongs, Bishop Dammert Bellido sums up this point succinctly, "He should be ready to give himself, according to the requirements of his priesthood and the spiritual needs of our countries."

The bishop has additional thoughts for missionaries from Spain. Even if language and many practices are the same, they must not overlook the differences. Catholicism has existed in Spain for nineteen centuries, in Latin America for only four. Many non-Spanish elements exist, some indigenous, others derived from French and Anglo-Saxon cultures. "You cannot treat the same a Peruvian raised in the debilitating climate of the Pacific, and a native of Old Castile or Navarre, whose strong physical constitution was ensured by the climate in which he was reared. . . . From the common Greco-Roman trunk sprang the different civilizations of Spain, France, Italy and other countries, each with its own characteristics; from the civilization of Spain likewise developed, each with its own special forms, the civilizations of America."

The missionary from the United States has been discussed with equal frankness. The conclusions of the first Inter-American Congress on Rural Life, held at Manizales, Colombia, include the following comments:

"Religious from the United States living in Latin America are often unable to profit fully from their contacts with Latin American culture. They do not find themselves well prepared to transmit the benefits of their own culture, because they lack an adequate grounding in the social sciences. Missionaries have long recognized the impossibility of appreciating a culture other than their own without specialized preparation.

"Not less important than the culture conflict is the profound clash between the urban mentality of religious from the United States and the rural society into which they are thrown, a clash that affects all their work as missionaries."

No doubt these frank criticisms reflect real experiences. If they do, I think United States missionaries in Latin America can be proud of the speed at which they are maturing. This is, of course, part of a wider movement, for mission techniques and a mission philosophy have developed at a phenomenal rate in the United States since World War II, a growth expressed in mission institutes and seminars, a thriving technical literature, a universal recognition of the need for specialized preparation, and a broad and enthusiastic exchange of experiences. The Maryknoll Fathers have been pioneers here, as in many fields, and I also think immediately of the training programs initiated by Msgr. Ivan Illich at the Catholic University of Puerto Rico, and the institutes for language and culture studies he now operates in Mexico and in Brazil for personnel of the United Nations, the Peace Corps, religious orders, lay missionary groups and others.

The United States missionary does create special problems in Latin America or wherever he works. He is backed by financial resources which differentiate him from his neighboring priests, whether native-born or from Europe. A personal level of living which represents to him a great sacrifice in relation to his background is for them an almost scandalous display of luxury. His approach to his work seems to some to place more emphasis on the card index than on divine grace.

In my experience, United States missionaries are properly conscious that they create such problems. Discussions I have had with them, with their priest neighbors and with their parishioners have convinced me that Bishop Larraín of Chile put the situation in proper perspective when he summed it up as follows. In principle, he told me, there is real danger of "costly and bitter failure," if United States missionaries fail to give adequate weight to the different historical and cultural factors which Catholicism in Latin America reflects.

In practice, however, he continued, "I think I can say that the problem is far from acute. There is a great and growing awareness among the missionary priests, brothers and sisters from the United States, now numbering several thousands, who are devoting their lives to helping us in Latin America, of the need for cultural accommodation to make their sacrifice fruitful. We recognize this and are grateful for it. And I can say the same of the splendid lay mission groups, like the Grail, the Association for International Development, and the Lay Mission-Helpers Association."

The same views were expressed in even more vigorous terms by a young, dynamic churchman from the highlands of Peru, Bishop Alcides Mendoza Castro. "I had only eleven priests in a diocese that needs a hundred and twenty," he told me. "Then Cardinal Cushing sent me twelve of his, and already they have worked a transformation which they themselves do not realize, in that they have introduced the possibility of a progress and a rebirth where none existed. I'm no longer afraid of Khrushchev. I'm no longer afraid of Castro. Their agitators succeeded because they filled a vacuum. The vacuum doesn't exist any more. These priests have filled it. They are God's blessing on my diocese."

Bishop Mendoza Castro was referring to a relatively new addition to the United States mission organizations in Latin America, the Society of St. James the Apostle, founded in 1959 by Cardinal Cushing of Boston, with the express intention of tapping what the Cardinal believes is a huge unexploited reserve of potential mission personnel. The Society accepts diocesan priests from the United States to work in Latin America for whatever length of time each chooses to stay. They remain under the jurisdiction of their own bishop and can go back when they want to, or when he recalls them. By late 1961, more than forty members were in charge of parishes in Bolivia and Peru.

The apostolate of these priests is based on the belief that the parish in Latin America must be built on a middle-class community capable of providing the economic basis for the functioning of schools and other community services, and engaged actively in the work of the parish through a sense of common effort and participation. This is very much the type of parish which exists in the United States, and very often in Latin America the work must begin entirely from scratch. I have already described one such effort in a mountain valley near Lima, where the pastor is in fact a member of the Society of St. James the Apostle.

In this approach the Society is only following in the footsteps of the Maryknoll Fathers, who are both in numbers and in geographic distribution the most important mission group from the United States in Latin America. The impact such a parish makes in as little as ten or twelve years has to be seen to be believed, with benefits visible at all levels. There is a vast improvement in attendance at church. The children who graduate from the schools have better economic opportunities because of the level of their education. Vocations become more numerous. Community organizations, including credit unions and cooperatives, spring up and flourish. People gain a sense of self-confidence. No other United States aid to Latin America produces such rapid and such dramatic results.

Conclusion

THE MOVE BY THE CATHOLIC CHURCH since World War II to identify itself with the aspirations of the masses in Latin America, to define and proclaim these aspirations, and to develop leadership for the masses, is probably the most significant of all the momentous happenings of those postwar years. It means that the strength of the Church as a social institution will no longer be available to the upper class to support its conservative aims. It means, too, that the masses will no longer be hamstrung by their previously irremediable defect, lack of leadership.

Nevertheless, for the reasons I have set out earlier, I think there is little likelihood that Latin America will develop along the same lines as the United States. The middle class is too small and weak, and it is pressed too violently from both ends, that is to say, by the still strong upper class and by the rapidly expanding proletariat. Classical middle-class democracy is likely to be short lived, wherever it succeeds in establishing itself, and the narrowness of its base will cause it to live in the permanent crisis that has characterized post-Perón Argentina, itself the most middle-class of the Latin American republics. Where it is not overthrown by reactionary forces, as has happened many times already, it will yield to new political forms in which the major power will be in the hands of the working class, and which will tend to pattern themselves along the lines of the west-Europe welfare state or the east-Europe dictatorship of the proletariat.

It is hard to see how the latter alternative can ultimately be avoided unless the massive investment of money and know-how needed to accelerate tremendously the regional rate growth is rapidly made available, thereby providing an internal dynamism greater and more rapid than the rate of population growth. When I say this, I am of course saying nothing new. The Eisenhower administration had reluctantly reached the same conclusion during its final year in office, and the Kennedy administration is totally dedicated to the same thesis, which is the motivation and justification for its Alliance for Progress program. With characteristic vigor, President Kennedy presented the alternatives in a speech delivered in March 1962, on the first anniversary of the Alliance offer.

Referring to the Charter of Punta del Este, which in August 1961 formalized Latin America's acceptance of the Alliance and its desire to promote peaceful revolution in the hemisphere, he said:

"That revolution had begun before the Charter was drawn. It will continue after its goals are reached. If the goals are not achieved, the revolution will continue but its methods and results will be tragically different. History has removed for governments the margin of safety between the peaceful revolution and the violent revolution. The luxury of a leisurely interval is no longer available."

Perhaps the greatest obstacle to success is the vacuum of moral and religious training which characterizes all of western civilization today, a condition exaggerated in Latin America by a century and a half of emotional divorce between the ruling classes and the region's one great religious institution, as well as by the low levels of education. The required material transformation can hardly be effected without a sense of high moral purpose. And such purpose is widely lacking. Instead, we find governments seeking to bolster devices like multiple exchange rates and deficit financing, while failing to use the time gained by such devices to remedy basic defects. A major part of national effort is diverted from productive activity to counter measures, such as illegal export of capital, double invoicing of imports, and smuggling on a massive scale. Even big and reputable firms throughout the area, both Latin American and North American, are involved in such transactions, which require wholesale bribery of public officials, falsification of official documents, and corruption at all levels.

Creation of a climate of public morality and honor is, accordingly, a primary need. But obviously, this is an area where outside help is of its nature limited. Nor would it be realistic to sit back and refuse technical and financial help until the housecleaning has been completed. The time schedule is too tight. Certainly, we in the United States, with our unresolved race conflict, for example, and a system of measuring national progress which equates expanded production of pornography with expanded production of steel, cannot presume to pose as guardian of Latin American morals. Or if we do, at least we should first confine ourselves to ensuring that our economic aid and business practices in Latin America are in themselves above suspicion and are calculated to support those elements which give the most promise of effecting the wished-for transformation of the region's public institutions.

The foregoing considerations combine with what has been said earlier about the ruling classes' inherent resistance to change to point up the danger of channeling aid to Latin America through existing government agencies and programs. Our own government is conscious of the dilemma, though it has not yet faced it squarely. Quite apart from the instability of governments, causing disruption of operation and alteration of direction with each violent change of rulers, there is the well-recognized fact of diversion of funds, the siphoning off of unconscionable business profits, and losses through poor administration, public and private.

On top of this, there is the further fact that the existing power structure ensures that benefits are concentrated in certain sectors of the economy. Technical reasons are invented to give excessive weight to the needs of international commerce, big industry, large-scale agriculture and mining, to lavish public works, the army and certain urban segments, to the neglect alike of the urban slum dwellers and of the landless peasants, who between them constitute three-quarters of the inhabitants of many countries.

The Kennedy administration started out on the assumption that it could eliminate the defects just described by imposing terms on Latin American governments in return for the aid it would offer them, and the signers of the Punta del Este Charter, namely, all the American republics except Cuba, accepted this principle. Its limitations, nevertheless, quickly became apparent. It proved easy for governments seeking to avoid compliance with conditions demanded by the United States (land reforms, tax reforms, accounting procedures, etc.) to apply counterpressures. It took almost no effort on their part to misrepresent Washington's intentions and to bring into action in their own countries an incongruous coalition of leftist, conservative and ultra-nationalistic elements to denounce the revival in a new guise of the historic interventions of Uncle Sam in the domestic affairs of his neighbors. Irresponsible statements by United States businessmen concerned only with profits, amplified by their spokesmen in Congress, helped to convince even the most favorably disposed Latin Americans of the truth of such charges.

Stalemated on this level, as it is, the United States might well give more attention to another channel of aid for Latin America which has already proved valuable to the extent to which it has been utilized, namely, provision of aid on a people-to-people level through counterpart voluntary agencies and institutions.

I am thinking, for example, of the possibility of massive expansion of programs by which a university in the United States undertakes the development of a university in a Latin American country. The selection could be made primarily by the institutions concerned, taking into account their specializations, interests, cultural contacts, and so on. Similar programs could be developed in all intellectual areas, including the practical professions, such as accounting and statistics, which urgently need upgrading at the expense of the traditional professions, especially law. Industry could likewise take the initiative in the transfer of know-how, even to the point of organizing its own teams of pioneers modeled on the Peace Corps, which has won immediate acceptance.

The major agencies and institutions for such people-to-people programs already exist in the United States, eliminating the need to build new bureaucracies to administer official programs. The fact that few counterpart organizations are to be found in the receiving countries, and that many of them exist mainly on paper, is not an argument against this approach. One of Latin America's great weaknesses comes from its long period of living under paternalistic systems. It has no experience of self-help and consequently lacks an inducement to develop self-help organizations. Providing the inducement would serve as a forced draft to speed their creation and give them the means to prove their worth quickly.

A people-to-people approach would further serve to bring home the basic fact that the problem of Latin America is a human problem. Too often it reaches us as a coffee surplus or a run-away inflation or a shortage of dollars. But these are mere phenomena. We can never begin to solve it until we recognize that we are dealing with people, human beings like ourselves, who want the simple essentials guaranteed us by the Constitution: the right to life, liberty and the pursuit of happiness, rights which technical progress places today within the reach of all but which many are unable to enjoy because of the failure of the systems under which they live.

Some Statistics

Area, population, productivity and mortality figures are from publications of the U. S. Department of Commerce, the International Monetary Fund and the United Nations. Population figures are mid-1960 estimates; most of the others are for 1959. The religious statistics for Latin American countries are from *Latin American Ecclesiastical Statistics*, 1960, published by The Maryknoll Fathers, and also reflect the estimates for 1959.

Per capita gross national product (sum of all goods and services produced in a given economy) figures are today regarded as giving a better picture of the level of development than per capita income figures. As a rule, per capita income would be 10 to 20 per cent lower. These figures are indicative rather than substantive. The data on which they are based are often defective, and the exchange rate used to convert to U. S. dollars introduces an additional variation. The figure for Cuba is 1958, after which date no figures are available. The U. S. gnp is for 1960.

ARGENTINA

Date of independence:	July 9, 1816
National hero:	José de San Martín
Area:	1,061,084 sq. mi.
Population:	20,956,000
Capital: Buenos Aires (metropolitan area)	5,600,000
Urban percentage of whole:	68%
Density per sq. mile:	20
Per capita gross national product:	US$343
Infant mortality rate (1958) per thousand live births:	61.1
Percentage of Catholics:	89%
No. of Catholics per priest:	4,100
Total priests:	4,859
Principal products:	meat, hide, wool, grains, milk products, timber

BOLIVIA

Date of Independence:	August 6, 1825
National hero:	Antonio José de Sucre
Area:	424,162 sq. mi.
Population:	3,462,000
Capital: La Paz	347,000
Urban percentage of whole:	37%
Density per sq. mile:	8
Per capita gross national product:	US$105
Infant mortality rate (1954) per thousand live births:	90.7
Percentage of Catholics:	93%
No. of Catholics per priest:	4,900
Total priests:	694
Principal products:	tin, lead, silver, tungsten, zinc, antimony, copper

BRAZIL

Date of independence:	September 7, 1822
National hero:	José Bonifacio de Andrada e Silva
Area:	3,270,224 sq. mi.
Population:	65,743,000
Capital: Brasilia	120,000
Major cities: São Paulo	3,674,000
Rio de Janeiro	3,124,000
Urban percentage of whole:	37%
Density per sq. mile:	21.5
Infant mortality rate (1957) per thousand live births:	107.5
Per capita gross national product:	US$331
No. of Catholics per priest:	5,557
Total priests:	10,616
Principal products:	coffee, rice, beans, cacao, diamonds

CHILE

Date of independence:	1818
National hero:	Bernardo O'Higgins
Area:	283,011 sq. mi.
Population:	7,627,000
Capital: Santiago	839,000
Urban percentage of whole:	66%
Density per sq. mile:	27
Per capita gross national product:	US$514
Infant mortality rate (1960) per thousand live births:	119.6
Percentage of Catholics:	90%
No. of Catholics per priest:	2,750
Total priests:	2,350
Principal products:	copper, saltpeter, tubers, wool

COLOMBIA

Date of independence:	1824
National hero:	Francisco de Paula Santander
Area:	439,521 sq. mi.
Population:	14,132,000
Capital: Bogotá	1,257,000
Urban percentage of whole:	48%
Density per sq. mile:	32
Per capita gross national product:	US$253
Infant mortality rate (1959) per thousand live births:	96.9
Percentage of Catholics:	90%
No. of Catholics per priest:	3,650
Total priests:	3,810
Principal products:	gold, platinum, coffee, emeralds, hides, textiles

COSTA RICA

Date of independence:	September 15, 1821
National hero:	Juan Rafael Mora
Area:	19,652 sq. mi.
Population:	1,171,000
Capital: San José	102,000
Urban percentage of whole:	36%
Density per sq. mile:	60
Per capita gross national product:	US$401
Infant mortality rate (1959) per thousand live births:	81
Percentage of Catholics:	88%
No. of Catholics per priest:	4,200
Total priests:	246
Principal products:	coffee, cacao, bananas, hemp, sugar

CUBA

Date of independence:	May 20, 1902
National hero:	José Martí
Area:	44,216 sq. mil
Population:	6,797,000
Capital: Havana	785,000
Urban percentage of whole:	55%
Density per sq. mile:	154
Per capita gross national product:	$410
Infant mortality rate ( ) per thousand live births:	
Percentage of Catholics:	89%
No. of Catholics per priest:	7,850*
Total priests:	723*
Principal products:	sugar, tobacco, fruits minerals

* 1959 figures. The Castro regime subsequently expelled very many priests. An NCWC despatch in May 1962 said only 120 priests were left.

DOMINICAN REPUBLIC

Date of independence:	February 27, 1844
National hero:	Juan Pablo Duarte
Area:	18,815 sq. mi.
Population:	3,014,000
Capital: Santo Domingo	367,000
Urban percentage of whole:	28%
Density per sq. mile:	160
Per capita gross national product:	$225
Infant mortality rate (1959 provisional) per thousand live births:	108
Percentage of Catholics:	98%
No. of Catholics per priest:	8,600
Total priests:	310
Principal products:	sugar, cacao, coffee, molasses, corn, tobacco

ECUADOR

Date of independence:	August 10, 1809
National hero:	Eugenio Espejo
Area:	101,911 sq. mi.
Population:	4,298,000
Capital: Quito	314,000
Urban percentage of whole:	34%
Density per sq. mile:	42
Per capita gross national product:	US$201
Infant mortality rate (1959) per thousand live births:	105.8
Percentage of Catholics:	98%
Number of Catholics per priest:	3,250
Total priests:	1,193
Principal products:	bananas, balsawood, cacao, coffee, gold, petroleum, rice

EL SALVADOR

Date of independence:	September 15, 1821
National hero:	José Matias Delgado
Area:	7,722 sq. mi.
Population:	2,612,000
Capital: San Salvador	231,000
Urban percentage of whole:	35%
Density per sq. mile:	338
Per capita gross national product:	US$208
Infant mortality rate (1959) per thousand live births:	78.1
Percentage of Catholics:	97%
No. of Catholics per priest:	7,600
Total priests:	277
Principal products:	coffee, vegetable oils, cotton, fabrics, gold, hemp, rice, silver, salt

GUATEMALA

Date of independence:	September 15, 1821
National hero:	Justo Rufino Barrios
Area:	41,004 sq. mi.
Population:	3,759,000
Capital: Guatemala City	385,000
Urban percentage of whole:	30%
Density per sq. mile:	92
Per capita gross national product:	US$178
Infant mortality rate (1959) per thousand live births:	89.7
Percentage of Catholics:	98%
No. of Catholics per priest:	11,000
Total priests:	279
Principal products:	coffee, bananas, resins, hemp, timber

HAITI

Date of independence:	January 10, 1804
National hero:	Jean-Jacques Dessalines
Area:	10,425 sq. mi.
Population:	3,505,000
Capital: Port-au-Prince	200,000
Urban percentage of whole:	17%
Density per sq. mile:	336
Per capita gross national product:	US$98
Infant mortality rate (1957) per thousand live births:	171
Percentage of Catholics	78%
No. of Catholics per priest:	5,950
Total priests:	450
Principal products	coffee, sugar, bananas, sisal, cotton, molasses, cacao

HONDURAS

Date of independence:	September 15, 1821
National hero:	Francisco Morazán
Area:	43,278 sq. mi.
Population:	1,953,000
Capital: Tegucigalpa	125,000
Urban percentage of whole:	25%
Density per sq. mile:	45
Domestic per capita product:	US$196
Infant mortality rate (1960) per thousand live births:	52
Percentage of Catholics:	97%
No. of Catholics per priest:	9,950
Total priests:	156
Principal products:	bananas, silver, gold, timber, livestock, cigars, tobacco, coconuts

MEXICO

Date of independence:	September 16, 1810
National hero:	Miguel Hidalgo y Costilla
Area:	760,335 sq. mi.
Population:	34,923,129
Capital: Mexico City (metropolitan area)	2,698,000
Urban percentage of whole:	50%
Density per sq. mile:	46
Per capita gross national product:	US$293
Infant mortality rate (1959) per thousand live births:	75.5
Percentage of Catholics:	96%
No. of Catholics per priest:	4,800
Total priests:	6,290
Principal products:	lead, coffee, silver, gold, fibers, resins, zinc, cotton, petroleum

NICARAGUA

Date of independence:	September 15, 1821
National hero:	Miguel Larreynaga
Area:	52,896 sq. mi.
Population:	1,475,000
Capital: Managua	191,000
Urban percentage of whole:	37%
Density per sq. mile:	28
Per capita gross national product:	US$210
Infant mortality rate (1959) per thousand live births:	64.2
Percentage of Catholics:	92%
Number of Catholics per priest:	4,550
Total priests:	222
Principal products:	coffee, cotton, gold, fibers, timber livestock, corn, rice

PANAMA

Date of independence:	November 3, 1903
National hero:	Tomás Herrera
Area:	28,753 sq. mi.
Population:	1,053,000
Capital: Panama City	253,000
Urban percentage of whole:	47%
Density per sq. mile:	37
Per capita gross national product:	US$369
Infant mortality rate (1958) per thousand live births:	60
Percentage of Catholics:	91%
No. of Catholics per priest:	5,200
Total priests:	171
Principal products:	bananas, fiber, cacao, coconut, hides

PARAGUAY

Date of independence:	May 14, 1811
National hero:	
Area:	157,046 sq. mi.
Population:	1,768,000
Capital: Asunción	281,000
Urban percentage of whole:	35%
Density per sq. mile:	11
Per capita gross national product:	US$120
Infant mortality rate (1958) per thousand live births:	54
Percentage of Catholics:	95%
No. of Catholics per priest:	5,250
Total priests:	313
Principal products:	cotton, meat extracts, quebrecho, timber, hide, maté, tobacco

PERU

Date of independence:	July 28, 1821
National hero:	Hipólito Unanue
Area:	482,258 sq. mi.
Population:	10,857,000
Capital: Lima	1,262,000
Urban percentage of whole:	41%
Density per sq. mile:	23
Per capita gross national product:	US$129
Infant mortality rate (1958) per thousand live births:	85
Percentage of Catholics:	97%
No. of Catholics per priest:	5,400
Total priests:	1,740
Principal products:	petroleum, copper, gold, lead, silver, zinc, cotton, sugar, wool, linen

URUGUAY

Date of independence:	August 25, 1825
National hero:	José Gervasio Artigas
Area:	72,174 sq. mi.
Population:	2,827,000
Capital: Montevideo	923,000
Urban percentage of whole:	81%
Density per sq. mile:	39
Per capita gross national product:	US$580
Infant mortality rate (1956) per thousand live births:	73
Percentage of Catholics:	90%
No. of Catholics per priest:	3,650
Total priests:	688
Principal products:	wool, livestock, meat extracts, grains and other agricultural products, hides and furs

VENEZUELA

Date of independence:	July 5, 1811
National hero:	Simón Bolivar
Area:	340,560 sq. mi.
Population:	6,709,000
Capital: Caracas	1,372,000
Urban percentage of whole:	61%
Density per sq. mile:	20
Per capita gross national product:	US$1,062
Infant mortality rate (1959) per thousand live births:	58.7
Percentage of Catholics:	88%
No. of Catholics per priest:	4,350
Total priests:	1,351
Principal products:	petroleum, coffee, cacao

LATIN AMERICA

Area (20 republics)	7,659,047 square miles
Population	198,344,000
Urban percentage of whole	46%
Density per square mile	26
Per capita gross national product	US $395
Infant mortality per thousand live births	91.5
Percentage of Catholics	92%
No. of Catholics per priest	4,750
Total priests	37,920

UNITED STATES

Area	3,555,491 square miles
Population [1]	185,186,000
Urban percentage of whole	70%
Density per square mile	51
Per capita gross national product	$2,750
Infant mortality per thousand live births	26.4
Percentage of Catholics [2]	23.69%
No. of Catholics per priest [2]	771
Total priests [2]	55,581

[1] U. S. Census Bureau estimate of Total Population as of Jan. 1, 1962.

[2] From *Official Catholic Directory*, 1962, published by P. J. Kenedy & Sons, N. Y.